THE SOMME BATTLEFIELD

A pocket guide to Places and People
with Secret Maps

Ruaraidh Adams-Cairns

Ruaraidh Adams-Cairns

HAYLOFT PUBLISHING LTD

First published by Hayloft Publishing Ltd., 2014

Hayloft Publishing Ltd, South Stainmore,
Kirkby Stephen, Cumbria, CA17 4DJ

tel: 017683 41568 or 07971 352473
email: books@hayloft.eu
web: www.hayloft.eu

Copyright © Ruaraidh Adams-Cairns, 2014

ISBN 978 190 452 4236

Designed, printed and bound in the EU

Papers used by Hayloft are natural, recyclable products made from wood grown in
sustainable forests. The manufacturing processes conform to the environmental
regulations of the country of origin.

For Susie.
Asking her to marry me was the cleverest thing I ever did.
Being accepted, the luckiest.

Acknowledgements

WHEN I FIRST visited the Somme and began by taking my family and friends, I never intended to assemble a book. I did, however, start making notes from books, articles, the internet and anything else which caught my attention. Now, over ten years later, as I assemble my notes into a short publication, there are many cases for which I can no longer remember where I sourced the material. Where I can, I have tried to make an appropriate acknowledgement. All those I have approached have been kind and generous in granting their consent for publication. In all or any cases where I have failed to acknowledge the source in an appropriate way, I hope the authors will grant me forgiveness.

I should particularly like to thank Jeremy Davidson, Gunner Price's grandson, and the late Peter Moore MC, the son of Aubrey Moore MC, for access to their family papers; Richard van Emden for allowing me to use *Famous 1914-1918* and *Last Man Standing*; David Raw for my reliance on *It's Only Me!*; Tricia Thorns and the producers of *My Real War 1914-?* for the last letter from Captain Len Havilland Le Mesurier and the numerous contributors to websites on whose material I have relied over the years.

I would also like to thank the Commonwealth War Graves Commission for their prompt and efficient response to questions and for allowing me to print the plan of Foncquevillers Military Cemetery, as well as Gavin Bartlet in Savills Drawing Office, who has done a wonderful job with the maps. I would also like to thank the Imperial War Museums and the Institut National de l'Information Geographie et Forestière for their help.

My special thanks go to James Kerr who is an established and admired photographer. I knew him over 30 years ago when we were both in the army. He approached me recently to ask if I would be interested in co-operating with him in producing an illustrated book on the Battle of the Somme. I explained that this book was ready to go to the publishers and he immediately, and very generously, offered me a selection of his wonderful photographs. Finally, I would like to thank my brother, Iain, for reading my text, correcting as much of my spelling as he could and suggesting many improvements.

Contents

The basilica in Albert has been rebuilt, but during most of the war the Madonna was hanging precariously in a horizontal position.

Introduction

LIKE MOST BRITS, several of my forbears fought in the Great War in France. My great uncle, Eugene Crombie, who had recently been a scholar at Winchester College, joined up in 1914. On arrival in France, he began a regular and almost daily postal correspondence with his mother, to whom he was very close.

He served on the Somme. He was wounded early in 1916, evacuated back to London for treatment, began his training as a barrister and fell in love. Once fully recovered, he returned to France, only to be killed at the Battle of Arras in April 1917. He was twenty years of age.

After his death, his mother had all his letters typed up and bound into two leather-covered books. They caught my imagination. I too had served in a Highland Regiment at the same age. His observations about his life at the front were both detailed and insightful. They led me back to the Somme to try and retrace his steps. As soon as I arrived there, I became captivated by the rolling expanse of chalk downs interspersed with copses and woods. It seemed a totally improbable setting for the awful horrors of the battle and the huge numbers of soldiers killed on its soil. It was also difficult to reconcile its desolate and abused condition, as described by my great uncle, with the beauty of the peaceful landscape I found.

I was also struck by the integrity of the battlefield itself. With the exception of the Commonwealth War Graves and a few specific monuments, the landscape today would be easily recognisable to the soldiers who first arrived there in 1914. The roads, villages and woods are all almost exactly where they were 100 years ago. In many cases, even the old trench lines and shell holes are still visible and unexploded munitions and shrapnel can be found in the fields.

I learned that the most moving way to visit the battlefield is to have an understanding of specific individuals' experiences at exact places on the battlefield. I discovered that there were lots of guide books but these seemed either to cover the entire area with comparatively little human detail, or to cover the ground and the tactical movement of troops over it, at huge length.

This book is accordingly an attempt to cover a few places in slightly greater detail by giving an insight into the people who served and, in many cases, sadly died there. Over the last ten years I have revisited the Somme on a regular basis and spent many hours trying to pin the exploits or experiences of particular individuals to spots on the battlefield, sometimes for the benefit of the individuals' descendants. This short book is a small collection of such stories with maps, hence the title.

I have tried to select specific parts of the battlefield and stories about individuals to enable me to touch on some of the other historical events which have become woven into our understanding of the war. I hope, taken as a whole, it will give a reasonable overview of this extraordinary battle.

This personal and pared down selection of places can all be visited within a couple of days. There is no need to visit all 20 places or follow the same order but I would recommend that you at least start at Place No. 1 and visit No. 2, as together they set the scene for much of what comes later. (If you are short of time then numbers 9, 12 and 13 should not be missed.)

I have included a map of the entire battlefield so that you should be able to find the places and then some larger scale trench maps so that you get a better feel for the frightening proximity of the enemy trenches. I have mainly relied on the original secret 1916 trench maps but I have had these over-printed with the subsequent cemeteries, as well as colouring the extent of the modern woods and power lines to assist more exact identification.

I hope this guide will offer a framework into which readers will be able to integrate their own forbears' experiences, either as armchair tourists or better still, as visitors to the battlefield itself with their own family and friends.

Anyone who visits the Somme will never either regret, or forget it.

Ruaraidh Adams-Cairns
London, 2014

The Background to the Battle of the Somme

AT THE BEGINNING of the twentieth century, the world was dominated by two economic and industrial super-powers, Great Britain and Germany. It was a period of huge industrial growth and wealth creation. It was accompanied by the growth and ambitions of empires. This led to fear. Germany felt threatened by Russia and France, France by Germany, Russia by Germany and the Austro-Hungarian Empire.

This fear in turn led to an arms race, with massive increases in expenditure. Germany, France and Great Britain all doubled their military budgets. Whilst Great Britain had a policy, as a naval power, of having a navy larger than the combination of the two next largest, it had one of the smallest armies of under 350,000 men. Germany reacted by expanding its navy but more significantly its army grew from 3 million to 4 million men. The other result of this fear was the establishment of a complex and secretive network of alliances. It was these alliances which ultimately led the world into war.

On 28th June 1914 Archduke Franz Ferdinand and his wife were assassinated by romantic nationalists trying to free Bosnia from the Austro-Hungarian Empire. The Emperor declared war on Serbia. Russia, an ally of Serbia, mobilized its army as a diplomatic initiative. Germany, whose defence policy had long rested on the Schlieffen Plan being an initial 'knock out' attack on France before turning on Russia, declared war on Russia and France. It invaded France through Belgium with a well-trained army of over 1.5m men. Britain had guaranteed Belgian independence in the Treaty of London (1839) so this action brought Britain into the war.

France responded by attacking into Alsace and Lorraine but was repulsed at a cost of over 300,000 French casualties. The French Army redeployed and managed to stop the German advance with an offensive on the River Marne. There then followed the so-called 'Race to the Sea' with each side trying to outflank the other; the final outcome saw the Germans withdrawing which enabled them to choose and establish their positions.

The Western Front became a line 475 miles long from Switzerland to the North Sea. 1915 proved to be the most murderous year of the entire war. It was the year of great offensives, all designed to achieve a 'breakthrough,' but all failed. In Turkey, British Empire troops made an unsuccessful attempt to attack the enemy's so-called soft underside, on the Dardanelles at Gallipoli.

In February 1916, the Germans attacked the French fortified positions at Verdun with the strategic objective of inflicting huge casualties. A massive German bombardment and a determined attack led to French casualties of over 700,000. These losses resulted in great political pressure on Great Britain to divert German forces away from Verdun and to mount a major joint offensive with the aim of 'breaking through' with a 'Big Push' and winning the war.

The French selected the River Somme for this offensive because at the southern end, it was a junction between French and British armies and it would enable the French to be involved. It was not General Haig's choice of ground, nor did he wish to attack at this time with his inexperienced, untested, and largely untrained new volunteer army. It was also to turn out that the majority of the promised additional French forces would fail to materialize.

The Germans had occupied the Somme in October 1914. They had chosen their ground with care, taking the high ground wherever possible. Their front line was a continuous strip of fortified villages and strongpoints, linked by three lines of trenches. In front of the trenches was a belt of barbed wire, perhaps three or four feet high and 20 or 30 yards deep. These obstacles represented the front line.

However, there were a further two lines of similar trenches to the rear which meant that the German trench network actually extended to a depth of up to five miles. For the Germans, the trench network was a defensive position which they intended to hold whilst they attacked Russia to the east. To this end, it was a semi-permanent structure and was supported by an extensive underground network of headquarters, sleeping quarters and hospitals dug into the chalk to a depth of up to 45 feet. Some of these quarters were concrete framed, timber lined and occasionally equipped with electricity.

The positioning of the front line enabled the Germans to sight the ground immediately to their front. This meant not only could they bring down accurate artillery fire on No Man's Land but also that the fire from their machine guns was either interlocking or overlapping, creating an effective killing zone to their front.

By contrast, the British trenches had been originally sited and dug by the French within sight of the German lines and in most cases on lower ground. They were of a comparatively temporary nature because they were only ever seen as a short term necessity. No Man's Land between the two front lines varied from several hundred yards to under fifteen yards at La Boisselle, where the troops could shout at each other. For any attacking infantry, the German line was a formidable obstacle. Furthermore, even if the front line could be captured, it would have to be defended quickly against a German counter-attack.

A trench is an open passage in the ground about eight feet deep. To enable troops to defend themselves, a platform known as a fire step was cut into the enemy facing wall, on which soldiers could stand to shoot over the top. If a trench was captured, it had to be 'reversed' and a fire step had to be quickly made on the opposite side, so that the soldiers could deal with any counter-attack from the other direction. This meant that the attacking troops had to carry all the equipment not only for attack but also for defence, in some cases up to about 60lbs a man.

The German troops occupying the Somme were either regular troops or experienced conscripts. This can be contrasted with the British soldiers who were mainly New Army troops. This was Kitchener's Volunteer Army which was raised in a rush on a local basis at the end of 1914, and which had been given a maximum of five months training before deployment to France. So the British, with inexperienced troops weighed down with equipment, were to attack seasoned soldiers, in exceptionally well-prepared defensive positions, uphill.

The British plan for the attack was extremely simple: first, smash their positions with artillery and underground mines; second, take their trenches with infantry and finally, attack through with cavalry.

The preparation and staff work for the attack was detailed and thorough. It lasted for months. In effect it was like building a city for a million people and two hundred thousand horses. New roads, bridges, railways, hospitals and airfields were built. New water supplies were laid on. The British occupied a front of about eighteen miles and 500 miles of telephone cable were laid for each mile of front.

Shells were stockpiled for a devastating bombardment. The objective of the bombardment was to destroy the German front line, sweep away the wire entanglements and knock out the German supporting artillery. It would last for seven days, involve 1,500 guns and use up to three million shells weighing 52 thousand tons. During the attack, the artillery would 'lift' their fire at regular intervals to more distant targets, as the British troops advanced.

Eighteen mines were dug under the German front line. This involved digging tunnels from the British lines under German strong-points and hollowing out caverns which were then filled with high explosive. One of the mines was to be the largest ever created with an explosion so loud that it would rattle the windows in Downing Street.

Once the infantry had taken the front line, the momentum of the attack would be maintained by the cavalry breaking through.

So confident was the General Staff of the success of this plan, but also so concerned that their inexperienced New Army troops might get out of control during the attack, that two disastrous decisions were made: first, the attack would go forward in broad daylight at 7.30am and second, the troops were ordered to walk.

The bombardment started on time and appeared to be highly effective.

Gunner Price, Royal Field Artillery (an Old Harrovian and Cambridge graduate who joined the ranks because of his stutter), explained:

The great bombardment began at 05:00 hours. We began firing High Explosive. In a few minutes the bombardment became intense. Other 18 pound batteries were doing "section fire ten seconds" which means that the two guns in the section fire independently, the second gun ten seconds after the first. Then the heavies opened up behind us.

The 18 pounders and the 4.5 guns made the most noise, their concussion seeming to hit the air everywhere with a ripping, tearing noise and made one feel as if you were being knocked sharply but painlessly about.

Gunner W. R. Price, by kind permission of Jeremy Davidson.

The firing miles away to the south sounded like a long dull roar but on the spot where we were, there were intervals between each gun firing of between a fraction of a second to three or four seconds. A pause of five seconds was rare. And so it went on, section fire with its regular firing, batteries with a persistent bang, bang, bang, salvos which tore the air with a birrip, birrip, birrip. 4.5s and 6 inch howitzers which barked sharply and severely, 8 inch howitzers, 6 inch naval guns and the 12 and 15 inch monsters whose shells seemed to plough their leisurely way over our heads, the burst reaching us much later, as a distant roar.

The Army's Royal Flying Corps had air superiority, and with wirelesses were able to direct artillery fire with accuracy. Buildings and villages were reduced to low heaps of rubble. Trenches were pulverized. German troops in the front line were disorientated and demoralized. They could not sleep or hear themselves talk. They were short of water and could not be re-supplied with food. They were cut off in their underground world and terrified that they would become entombed. Unfortunately, the weather worsened with low cloud and drizzle. Air observation became impossible and artillery observation limited.

British munitions factories were only just getting into full production and there were manufacturing faults. As many as 30% of the shells failed to explode. In addition, the half trained gunners of the New Army did not always set the fuses accurately. Many of those shells which did explode, burst too high to have any effect. There were too few heavy howitzers to destroy the Germans' deep dugouts. Artillery and machine gun emplacements were not destroyed.

Despite patrols exploring No Man's Land during the bombardment and reporting that the wire had not been cut, there was a general assumption from the visible devastation that the bombardment had done its job. One of the principles of attack is surprise. With a seven day bombardment it was clear to the Germans that an attack was imminent! The only question was when?

The hope of this remaining unknown was shattered by two events. First of all, at this stage in the war, Britain was using a wire communication system which utilized the ground as the 'earth connection'. This meant that the Germans were able to tap into British communications comparatively easily. An ill-disciplined British 'Good luck' message on the evening of 30th June alerted the Germans to the forthcoming attack. The second event was the decision on the timing of the detonation of the mines. It was decided that one of the larger mines would be detonated ten minutes before the attack on 1st July 1916 at 7.20am.

This mine effectively announced to the Germans the start of the attack. As soon as the British artillery lifted their fire from the German front trenches, they had time to come up from their dug-outs, man their parapets, set up their machine guns and get ready for the first wave of 60,000 soldiers who started walking towards them in lines 50 yards apart. They then called down artillery fire from their own artillery batteries, which had not been destroyed.

The losses were devastating. The British Army suffered 57,470 casualties of whom 19,240 were killed. It was, and remains, the single biggest loss of life which the British Army has ever sustained on a single day. The war lasted for 1,559 days and the British Empire suffered an average attrition rate of 582 deaths a day (908,000 were killed out of a total mobilised force of 8.9 million – less than half the attrition rate of France). So 19,240 was 33 times the average daily rate.

Attacking tends to incur higher casualties than defence and this was certainly true here. The German casualties on the same day are believed to have been fewer than 6,000.

To put these casualties in some sort of context, the British Army is

The Thiepval Memorial to the Missing.

thought to have lost fewer than 8,500 killed in the Battle of Waterloo which lasted a single day. This was very costly when compared to El Alamein – 1,112 over eleven days (about 100 a day). On Omaha beach on D Day in 1944, the Americans lost just over 500. In Iraq there were 179 over six years (29 a year) and in Northern Ireland, 768 over 38 years (20 a year).

The battlefield on the evening of 1st July can be described in two parts, divided by the arrow-straight road which runs from Albert to Bapaume through La Boisselle. North of the road and at La Boisselle, no gains had been made whatsoever. South of La Boisselle, although casualties were still high, a more intense barrage, better cut wire, less well defended positions and more imaginative leadership led to most of the first day objectives being captured.

It is open to speculation as to the alternative outcome which might have been achieved if General Rawlinson had deployed the cavalry to exploit the initiative as Haig had originally commanded. It is not clear why he did not do this but it is perhaps a reflection of his 'Bite and Hold' strategy as an infantry officer, in contrast to Haig's vision as a cavalryman.

The battle officially came to a close in November 1916 when the weather and ground conditions made further attacks impossible, although fighting actually continued on the Somme for most of the war. The total numbers of British and Commonwealth dead on the Somme in 1916 are uncertain but are certainly in excess of 200,000.

In judging the First World War today, it is easy to question the huge human cost. This is legitimate, but we should not overlook or fail to be deeply impressed by the British achievement in assembling, equipping and training an army which was ultimately responsible for defeating one of the best fighting forces the world had ever known.

PLACE ONE (Map A, page 148)

The Disastrous Diversionary Attack on Gommecourt Park

The extreme northern end of the offensive on 1st July 1916.

THE GROUND

Park your car in the narrow parking area in front of the Commonwealth War Cemetery known as Gommecourt Wood New Cemetery and then climb the steps in order to get a better view of the ground looking over the road. (I will not tell you about this graveyard because I want to cover Cemeteries in some detail at Place Two. This having been said, the isolated grave stones along the two outside walls which do not mark graves are of interest.)

Gommecourt – looking north between the two front lines

You are standing almost in the middle of No Man's Land. On your right is a wood known to the British as Gommecourt Wood. The front German trenches were about 200 yards to your right, crossing the road where it kinks and connects with the minor lane. The second line ran midway between this and the wood and the third line ran along the edge of the wood itself.

About 1,500 yards to the north east, the German line protruded forward and was known to the British as the Z, where there was a German machine gun post. It was capable of shooting at and killing anyone crossing the ground to your front.

The British front trench was slightly to your left just in front of the line of the pylons, although this had been dug simply as a jumping-off point and it was connected to the proper front line about 150 yards further back by a series of communication trenches sometimes known as Saps. Both the Saps and the jumping-off trench had been dug over the previous few weeks. Because of the nature of the soil, which is clay and loam over chalk, and the heavy rain, this had been a wet and tiring exercise with the Saps flooding and troops returning to the rear areas before dawn, caked in wet mud and exhausted from their exertions. Almost directly in front of you was the shelled remains of a sugar beet pad.

The story here concerns a Sap which was protruding from the main British front trench about 150 yards away from you to the north, close to a communication trench named Leicester Street, and the attack over the ground to your front, first by the Staffords and behind them 5th Leicesters. Beyond the Staffords to the north east, closer to the Little Z, were the Sherwood Foresters.

Behind you Gommecourt Wood bent around to the south east; this point was known as the Kaiser's Oak, being the furthest west the Germans had advanced. Gommecourt was one of the best defended positions on the Somme. There was an extensive network of trenches and deep dugouts, all protected by thick wire and twelve machine gun posts.

THE SITUATION ON 1ST JULY 1916

Gommecourt was to be the fulcrum of the whole attack, with no advance anticipated at this point. There were, however, three objectives: first to pinch out this kink in the British front line; second as a diversionary attack to absorb enemy troops and draw their attention away from the attack

Acting Captain Aubrey Moore, MC, 5th Leicestershire Regiment, at his wedding in September 1917. Photograph by kind permission of the late Peter Moore, MC.

further south; and third to protect the British flank to the south, as it advanced.

In order to achieve the first objective, there was to be an encircling attack with 46th (North Midland) Division, which included the Staffords, the Leicesters, and the Sherwood Foresters attacking from the north west (where you are standing) while the 56th (London) Division attacked from the south (a division contained about 18,000 men). The aim then was that the two divisions would link up east of Gommecourt.

In order to achieve the second objective of a diversion from the main attack to the south, preparations for assault here were deliberately made obvious. New trenches were dug while to the rear, headquarters, roads, light railways and new water supplies were all constructed. These works so caught the Germans' attention that they reinforced their position and made preparations so that the artillery from three of their divisions could be deployed to bring down defensive fire on the attackers.

While the 56th Division to the south had the advantage of well cut wire to their front, this was not the position at Gommecourt. The attempts to cut the wire or neutralise the German artillery had been undermined at this end of the line by a shortage of ammunition, which had been limited to 20 shells per gun.

AUBREY MOORE

Aubrey Moore was the son of a rector in Leicestershire. His uncle was the squire of the nearby village. He left school at 16 and qualified as a Mine Surveyor. In December 1913 he was commissioned into the 5th Leicestershire Regiment, which was a Territorial unit, rather than one of the later New Army battalions.

The Battalion was deployed to France in February 1915 and with his mining experience, Moore was appointed mining officer. He proved very successful and at Messines Ridge near Ypres, he was responsible for the digging of two tunnels up to the German line where he first located and then blew up German tunnels coming towards the British front. He subsequently built a defensive gallery against German tunnelling along the British front. For his perseverance and bravery he was awarded an MC, which was later presented to him at Buckingham Palace.

In March 1916, his Company Commander was killed by a trench mortar shell and he took over command of the Company as an Acting Captain.

He was 23 years old. In June 1916 the 5th Leicesters took over the position facing the German trenches here at Gommecourt, with a reserve position at Souastre, the next village to the west of Foncquevillers.

Acting Captain Moore, MC:
The German wire was hard and tough steel, much thicker than barbed wire used by farmers to restrain cattle. Barbs were one and a half to two inches long. These were very sharp and capable of giving a nasty tear to the flesh. If one got caught up in it, it was hard work to get free.

The wire was held up by wooden stakes, the depth of this carpet was seldom less than 20 yards and it was about three feet high. It was very dense. In the more strategic positions like Gommecourt the Germans had put down a double row.

Neither the British or French ever had wire defences comparable to the German wire. Not only did they wire us out but they wired themselves in.

On 1st July at about 7.30am we set off along a lane and into a communication trench up which we were to advance. The noise of the heavy shelling was terrible and any conversation meant shouting. The guns were firing a mixture of Smoke and High Explosive in addition to which a smoke trench mortar screen was put down. I was leading, my Company Sergeant Major Johnson was next and then came the commander of the leading platoon, a very young officer named William Callard from Leicester.

From my own army service I am aware of the difference and importance of the relationship which would have existed between these three individuals. An infantry battalion operates on a dual officer and non-commissioned officer basis. At the top of a battalion, the Commanding Officer has as his opposite number, the senior non-commissioned officer in the form of the Regimental Sergeant Major. At Company level, the Company Commander has a Company Sergeant Major and at Platoon level, a young officer is supported by a Sergeant. Each party is dependent on the other to be effective and close relationships are established as a result.

The Company Commander is the direct boss of the Platoon Commander and is responsible when a new platoon commander arrives for delegating an appropriate platoon sergeant to the young officer. I can still remember my own Company Commander explaining to me when I arrived, "A weak Platoon Commander needs a strong Platoon Sergeant. A strong Platoon Commander needs a very strong Platoon Sergeant!"

So the relationship we have here is that of the close working relationship between the Company Commander and his Company Sergeant Major and the more dependant relationship of the newly joined officer with his immediate superior, which is perhaps more akin to a new boy and a school monitor or prefect.

Acting Captain Moore, MC:

We had a very clear walk without any stops. When we were nearly at the front line, in front of which was a jumping-off trench, we came up to the tail end of the Stafford Company we were supporting which had stopped. One of their officers was there and I talked to him about the chance of success. At this point a shell hit the top of the trench above my head with the most almighty crash.

I was only aware of a vicious hit on my back from a clod of earth. I shouted, 'Come on' and went on after the Staffords. From this point I have no clear recollection of what happened.

Possibly two hours on, I found myself about 100 yards in front of our front line but short of the jumping-off trench sitting in a shell hole. I had no idea of how I got there or if I had gone over the parapet with the Staffords.

After a while I saw what looked like two men walking arm in arm. It turned out to be two Stafford officers who joined me in the shell hole. They were very shaken. By now I realised that I had been stunned by the shell burst which I dimly remembered. We talked and they explained that by the time they had reached the Boche wire they had few men left. Hundreds were either dead or wounded and the whole area was littered with bodies.

We eventually walked back to our line which we entered by the sap. I could see nothing of my own troops. My head was now fairly clear so I gave myself a metaphorical kick up the bottom and pulled myself together.

I located my position, went in the most likely direction and found some of my company mixed up with all sorts of men. I now learnt the terrible news that the shell which had nearly hit me had killed both

Company Sergeant Major Johnson and William Callard.
How it had hit them and not me I do not know. Johnson was only about three feet behind me and Callard was only that far from Johnson.
It was a terrible shock to me. Johnson was one of the best men, certainly a potential officer and Callard had shown great promise. It was tragic that he had had no previous trench experience; it must have been a ghastly ordeal for him to face shelling of that type for the first time.

The attack had got off to a bad start due to a large amount of rain over the previous 48 hours which had waterlogged many of the trenches and collapsed others. Some troops had spent the night up to their waists in mud and water. The attacking troops were short of sleep as a result of a further training exercise, which had been arranged when the attack was postponed, and the wet weather which had made sleep more difficult.

The wire which had been cut by the artillery was mainly repaired during the previous night. Although 'Smoke' had been put down by the artillery at the start of the attack, most of it had blown away after the first half of the Staffords had entered No Man's Land, thereby revealing the whole of the attack. This enabled the machine gun in the Z to the north to add fire to the fire coming from the front.

In front of the sugar beet pad, the German wire was still strong and as the troops struggled through, the enemy machine guns which were undamaged by the bombardment began inflicting huge losses.

Further north the Sherwood Foresters, who had led the Division attack on that side, managed to enter the wood and pressed on, leaving the first enemy lines to the next wave of troops. Then the German artillery opened up, effectively putting paid to the attack. The leading troops from the Sherwood Foresters who had fought through the front line were never seen again.

One VC was awarded to Captain Green who was the medical officer to the Sherwood Foresters. His citation read:

For Valour and most conspicuous devotion to duty. Although himself wounded, he went to the assistance of a young officer who had been wounded and was hung up in the enemy's wire entanglements. He succeeded in dragging him to a shell hole, where he dressed his wounds, notwithstanding that bombs and rifle grenades were thrown at him the whole time. Captain Green then endeavoured to bring the wounded officer into safe cover, and nearly succeeded in doing so when he himself was killed.

The young officer he was helping died three days later.

Within the 46th Division attacking this side of the wood, there were a total of 2,455 casualties. Five battalion commanding officers were killed or wounded. All 24 officers in the 5th Sherwood Foresters were casualties. The attack on Gommecourt cost a total of 2,765 killed or missing. The Germans lost 427.

The Divisional Commander, Major-General Montague-Stuart-Wortley, refused to mount a second attack later in the day because he could see it was pointless. The wood was entirely in German hands by 9.30pm. It was considered that the Division had showed a lack of offensive spirit and the Divisional Commander was duly relieved of his command.

Gommecourt was never captured by the Allies. It was only taken when the Germans gave it up during their retreat to the Hindenburg line in February 1917.

PLACE TWO (Map A, page 148)

Foncquevillers Military Cemetery and the Perfection of the War Graves

THE GROUND
There is space to park your car next to the Cemetery. Foncquevillers was known to the British troops as 'Funky Villas'. It had survived comparatively unscathed, partly as a result of the fact that before the British arrived, French and German troops had followed a policy of 'live and let live.'

At the time of the attack on 1st July 1916, the village was criss-crossed by support trenches and saps, many of which went under houses. The crypt under the church was a bomb store, with working parties arming shells with detonators, and an advanced dressing station had been established to treat the expected wounded.

THE COMMONWEALTH WAR GRAVES COMMISSION
On the outbreak of the First World War, Fabian Ware, a director of Rio Tinto, the large mining company, and a former editor of the *Morning Post*, found that at 45 he was too old for the British Army. He joined the British Red Cross and volunteered to go to France. On arrival in 1914 he was struck by the lack of any official mechanism for the permanent marking of graves and felt compelled to rectify the position.

In due course, thanks to his determination and vision, and with the support of the War Office, who recognised that the proper treatment of the bodies of dead soldiers would benefit the morale

Fabian Ware.

of those still fighting, the Imperial War Graves Commission was constituted through Royal Charter in 1917 (amending its name to Commonwealth in 1960). It was made up of six member states – the United Kingdom, Australia, Canada, India, New Zealand and South Africa.

THE LAND ON WHICH THIS CEMETERY STANDS IS THE FREE GIFT OF THE FRENCH PEOPLE FOR THE PERPETUAL RESTING PLACE OF THOSE OF THE ALLIED ARMIES WHO FELL IN THE WAR OF 1914 – 1918 AND ARE HONOURED HERE

A report was prepared for Parliament making two recommendations: first, no bodies should be repatriated because this would conflict with the feeling of brotherhood which had developed between all serving ranks – all the dead should be buried as brothers in arms on the battlefield; second, the memorials should avoid any class distinctions.

Both of these recommendations aroused heated debate within the country as well as in the House of Commons but were finally accepted. The Commonwealth War Grave Commission's mandate was to commemorate all Commonwealth war dead, individually, equally and in perpetuity.

The selected advisers were all leaders in their own fields. For example, the architects included Sir Edwin Lutyens; the gardens were the responsibility of Gertrude Jekyll and Rudyard

A typical wrought iron gate to a cemetery.

Kipling handled the words. They were clear in their vision and established that there would be two principles: permanence in physical form and perfection in appearance.

There was to be nothing to represent triumph, heroism or victory. The headstones are all identical so that there should be no difference for rank, race or creed. They are differentiated only by their inscriptions (the font design was specially commissioned), the national emblem or regimental badge, rank, name, unit, date of death and age, together with an appropriate religious symbol.

In the case of burials of Victoria Cross recipients, the regimental badge is augmented by the Victoria Cross emblem. In those cases where the casualty could not be indentified, the stone bears only those details discovered from the body. These graves are marked 'Known unto God'.

Each cemetery boundary is marked by a wall at least nine inches high and with the top parallel to the horizon. Today there are over 50 miles of such walls on the Somme. The ground on which cemeteries stand has been given by the people of France to their allies.

The Commonwealth War Grave Commission's undertakings began in

The Cross of Sacrifice designed by the architect Reginald Blomfield.

earnest at the end of the First World War. They recruited from the willing ranks of ex-servicemen who undertook the harrowing and often dangerous task of combing the battlefield in an attempt to locate lost corpses, as well as re-interring their pals from isolated or small graveyards into the larger cemeteries which were being built or extended.

They looked for bodies using long metal rods which they pushed into the ground, then pulled out and smelt. If the metal had come in contact with a corpse, the smell was distinctive. The cemetery building and grave concentration programme was completed in 1938, just before the outbreak of the Second World War.

Today the Commonwealth War Graves Commission cares for the graves and memorials of almost 1.7 million Commonwealth servicemen and women who died in both world wars and maintains graves and memorials at some 23,000 locations in over 150 countries. It is funded by grants from the six member states, with the majority coming from the United Kingdom. It is the first vote of a new Parliament and is currently in excess of £43 million per annum.

The Stone of Remembrance designed by Edwin Lutyens.

All the graveyards are different, stunningly attractive and unbelievably well maintained. They are all perfect. The Foncquevillers Cemetery is a good example of the War Grave Commission's work. It includes the following specific and typical features: an entrance gateway, with a wooden gate here, but often in wrought iron; here, and in cases where there are more than 40 graves, there is a Cross of Sacrifice designed by the architect Reginald Blomfield. It comprises a simple cross with an embedded bronze broadsword mounted on an octagonal base to represent the faith of the majority.

At Foncquevillers Cemetery, and normally in instances where there are over 1,000 graves, there is also a Stone of Remembrance. This was designed by Sir Edwin Lutyens. It is based on studies of the Parthenon with a plain geometry. The human eye perceives vertical sides and a

Sir Edwin Lutyens.

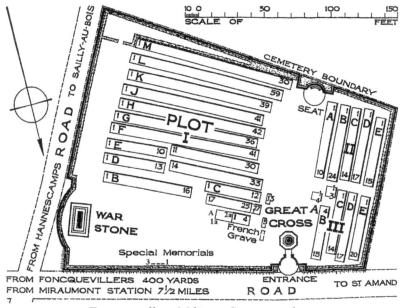

Foncquevillers Military Cemetery plan.

German soldier.

Chinese Labour Corps.

horizontal surface when neither is in fact the case. It is intended to com-memorate those of all faiths and those of none. It always stands on a plinth of three steps with the top and lower treads twice the width of the middle.

This cemetery also has several German graves which are distinguished by a pointed rather than a rounded top to the gravestone, some graves of Chinese Labour Corps workers and some Royal Canadian Air Force graves from the Second World War.

Specific graves you might like to visit are CSM Frank Johnson (I-L-14) and 2Lt William Callard (I-L-16) who were killed by the same shell during the attack on Gommecourt (William Callard shares his grave stone with two others) and Captain John Green (III-D-15), whose grave correctly has his VC emblem depicted.

Families were contacted and invited to provide inscriptions (for which they had to pay three and a half old pennies a letter).

Perhaps one of the most moving inscriptions is to be found on Private George Palmer's grave in Section II Row C grave 11. I think of it as a mother's prayer. It says: 'Will some kind hand in a foreign land place a flower on my son's grave.'

PLACE THREE (Map B, page 149)

Rossignol Wood and the Vicar's Victoria Cross

The Reverend Theodore Hardy V.C., D.S.O., M.C., the most highly decorated non-combatant of the First World War.

THE GROUND

Park your car on the west side of the wood off the road. The old German trenches are clearly visible in the wood as well as numerous shell holes. Follow the southern edge of the wood until you see the concrete remains of a German pillbox.

THE SITUATION IN APRIL 1918

You are standing in a field where in 1918 there was German wire. German barbed wire was thicker than English wire and the barbs were much longer. It was vicious stuff.

The soil here is a heavy clay over chalk and today it will not take you long to find pieces of old shrapnel. The pillbox formed part of the German defensive system which included three lines of trenches known to the British as Duck, Swan and Owl. Beyond Owl (but no longer visible), the line of the road was different and in something of a cutting.

Life in the open trenches by this stage in the war was inhuman. The trenches had become infested with rats, some of which grew as large as small cats on the unexpected supply of dead bodies and human waste. Lice quickly invaded soldiers' hair and clothing, causing men to scratch and twitch involuntarily. It was impossible to keep dry in a trench. There was no shelter or protection from the elements above, and cloying muddy water seeped up from below. When the sun came out, or the weather became drier and warmer, the smells worsened and were accompanied by clouds of flies.

The British positions and line of attack were from the north west along the contour line from the direction of Gommecourt. Their objective was to capture the three lines of trenches, with the sunken section of the road being the final objective.

Today the setting is green and peaceful. In 1918 the landscape was scarred by four years of war and the prominent colour of the ground and the woods was brown. In the background there was always the noise of gunfire and explosions and the awful smell of rotting human flesh.

THEODORE HARDY

Theodore Hardy was born in 1863, so he was 51 when the First World War began. He was brought up in London and attended London University before becoming a schoolmaster, first at Nottingham High School where he taught D. H. Lawrence.

He was popular with the boys and very keen on cricket but owing to his poor eyesight, he wore thick glasses; he was quite useless with a bat. Always deeply religious, he was ordained in 1898. In 1913 his beloved wife became terminally ill. He resigned his head-mastership and took over the living of a church in Lancashire. His wife died the following year.

On the outbreak of war, Hardy immediately volunteered to become an

The remains of the German pillbox.

Army Chaplain but was turned down on account of his advanced years. Frustrated, he decided to volunteer as a stretcher-bearer and attended and passed an ambulance course. He persisted in his efforts to get to the front and was eventually accepted as an Army chaplain in 1916, 4th Class, known as a padre, the devastation of the Somme having produced both a shortage of soldiers and of padres.

He was posted to the 8th Lincolns. At first, neither the officers nor men took much notice of Hardy. He was short of stature, quiet and self-effacing. Then they noticed he was different. He tended to sleep during the day and then take sweets and cigarettes up to the troops in their trenches at night.

He talked to them, read to and wrote letters for them. Then he took to assisting with the night ration run (a difficult, tiring and often dangerous undertaking). Finally, he started joining patrols and attacks, either to help with the wounded or to administer to the dying. He drove himself relentlessly and was often found asleep in the open, too exhausted to find shelter from the weather, or shell fire. When he discovered the neighbouring Battalion of Somerset Light Infantry had lost their padre, he adopted them too. It doubled his work load.

Rossignol Wood Cemetery which has more German graves than British.

His fearlessness and devotion to the men, combined with his quiet manner, won the respect and admiration of the entire Division. He became a cherished and much loved friend, lifting the troops' morale when he bumbled into their trenches with his catch phrase 'It's only me'. The men nicknamed him the 'Unkillable One'.

On 5th April 1918, Hardy's two battalions, the Lincolns and the Somersets, mounted an attack. Zero Hour was 5.30am.

The attack started well. A creeping barrage and smoke cover had been provided and the troops advanced behind eleven tanks, although most of them had broken down or been put out of action before reaching the first of the German trenches.

The initial attacks on Duck and Swan Trenches were successful and they were both captured and held. Owl Trench at the rear proved more resilient. At 9am, lorries full of German reinforcements were seen travelling towards the wood from the south-east and by midday they mounted a successful counter-attack, driving a wedge into the British front and forcing a withdrawal.

Hardy had taken part in the attack but hearing groans of pain coming from the German wire in front of Rossignol Wood, he had not withdrawn with the other troops but instead crawled back, under enemy fire, to see if he could help.

Later in the day as dusk approached, speculation was growing in the British Lines that the old man they called the 'Unkillable One' would not be returning. Then a small, but familiar figure, without his coat, was seen coming towards them from the enemy lines in the wood. He asked for a volunteer to go back with him to rescue a young wounded officer who was caught up in the German wire.

THE YOUNG OFFICER'S STORY:

I was alone; the others had had to leave me when the Germans counter attacked. My leg had felt numb at first, but then it began to hurt and throb. My blood was mixing with the chalky mud. 'Rather strange,' I thought, just like putting jam on rice pudding at school. School, I thought about school, they would be putting up the cricket nets again in Taunton.

I wondered what it would be like to die, and I expected to find out. In truth it didn't really seem to matter anymore. I was cold. I had lain here since six o'clock that morning, caught up in the German wire.

'It's only me!' he said, 'Keep quiet and still, they are back in the pill box again.'

I knew that voice. It was the padre, dear Old Hardy. I felt a tightening around my thigh as something was tied around it. I felt an arm around my shoulder and a warm coat being pulled over me.

We talked in whispers. The old man told me he used to go down to the Oval to watch W. G. Grace bat when he was a school boy. He asked me if I had played cricket at school. I told him I had, but that I did not suppose I would ever play cricket again with a leg like this. 'Course you will!' he said, 'but anyway you can't do worse than me, I always got a duck!'

We could hear the Germans talking and laughing in the pillbox. Either they thought I was dead or they were not looking at me. My teeth were chattering and my body was shaking. I could not understand what they were saying. I only did Latin and Greek at school.

I must have passed out because I became aware that it was nearly dark. 'Ssh…' I heard, 'It's only me. I'm still here but I am going to get help. I'll be back soon. You have done really well. Just hang on a bit longer.' Then I felt an arm lift off my back, and the cold of the night where before there had been the warmth of the old man's body.

I was frightened to be left alone unable to move. But I knew that the old man would come back, and that nothing, absolutely nothing, would stop him.

He did come back. The dear old padre and a tough old sergeant, each old enough to be my father. I knew what the padre would say before he said it, 'It's only me!' Then the sergeant snipped the wire with his wire cutters, deadening the sound with a cloth. It was like being a child again, being carried back by those two old men.

I was told later that the sergeant was awarded the Distinguished Conduct Medal. Then I was told that when the colonel had told the padre he was to get the VC he had replied, 'I knew nothing of what was going on in No Man's Land while I was attending your officer. I really think I ought to put in a protest!' but he didn't, because the colonel pointed out to him that this would only serve to advertise himself all the more.

Reverend Theodore Hardy V.C., D.S.O., M.C.

This was the first of three mentions of bravery in the citation for the VC which Hardy received that month. Whenever senior officers asked Hardy who should be decorated, Hardy was always keen to recommend others, but whenever the situation was investigated, it was always discovered that it was Hardy himself who was most deserving.

When talking to soldiers, he used to hold his left arm in such a way as to hide the ribbons on his chest. He showed no pride in them, quite the reverse. Hardy was appointed Chaplain to the King. The King and others became worried about him, the risks he was taking and the impact on morale if he was killed, so they tried to persuade him to accept a 'safe posting' in his home county. Hardy would have none of it. It turned out that he was not 'Unkillable.' He was wounded and died a month before the end of the war.

PLACE FOUR (Map C, page 150)

Sheffield Memorial Park and Kitchener's Pals Battalions

THE GROUND

Park your car by Serre Road No 1 Commonwealth War Grave Cemetery (Place No 5) and then walk up to Mark Copse (the Sheffield Memorial Park) on foot.

Stand at the south end of the wood. You will see the remains of the old British Line just inside the wood. This was the jumping-off point for the troops. Their line of attack was up the hill towards Serre, which is the village on the near horizon.

THE SITUATION IN JULY 1916

On 1st July 1916 there were no woods. There had been four copses known to the British as Matthew, Mark, Luke and John. All four had been completely demolished by enemy gun fire and the ground over which the troops were to attack was covered by high grass and scarlet poppies which hid numerous shell holes. (Today, not only have the copses re-established themselves but Mark, Luke and John have merged into one, part of which is now preserved as the Sheffield Memorial Park.)

A narrow gauge railway had been laid along the bottom of the small valley behind the front line, but in dead ground out of sight of the Germans, to bring ammunition and supplies forward. To the rear and slightly to the south was a wood known as Basin Wood, which had been chosen as a first aid post for soldiers wounded in the attack. The German front line was about 200 yards up the slope of the hill towards Serre.

THE THREE BRITISH ARMIES

On 1st July 1916 Great Britain had in effect three different armies on the battlefield. All three, in contrast to the German army, were volunteers. There were battalions from the regular army, well trained, well

The copses – Matthew, Mark, Luke and John, now merged into one.

disciplined and led by a distinctive and class sensitive officer class. They were in every sense a professional corps.

Next there were the Territorials (like the 5th Leicesters at Gommecourt) who were 'Part-Time Soldiers' recruited locally, based on local drill halls and trained in the evenings, weekends and over a fort-night's summer camp once a year. The officers were typically members of the local gentry but they were supported by a regular Adjutant, Regimental Sergeant Major and some Non-Commissioned Officers.

Finally, there was the New Army or Service Battalions, raised by Field Marshal Lord Kitchener in the latter part of 1914. Kitchener had been appointed as Secretary of State for War on the outbreak of war. He cor-rectly assessed both the likely duration of the war and the need for Great Britain to recruit a very much larger army in an extremely short period of time. His solution was not to expand either the Regular Army or the Territorials but instead to tap into a mixture of local civic pride, nation-al patriotism and a sense of belonging to a community, while utilising the infrastructure of the existing Regular Army.

These battalions were known as the Pals Battalions because groups of friends from the same street, football team or place of work, all joined up together.

Huge numbers (averaging 30,000 a day by the end of August 1914) had enlisted in a patriotic fervour, desperate to serve their country before the war came to an anticipated early end.

The 11th East Lancashires, known as the Accrington Pals, were raised in August and September 1914 as a result of the War Office accepting the Mayor of Accrington's offer to raise such a unit. Officers were initially nominated by the mayor irrespective of their military experience. Those who did have military experience were generally veterans, some of whom, including the Commanding Officer, were over 60 years of age.

Much of 1915 was spent being equipped and trained (during which time some of the older officers (including the Commanding Officer) were replaced), before being despatched to guard the Suez Canal for three months before being posted to the Somme.

THE ATTACK ON SERRE

The attack on Serre was characterized by being led by Pals Battalions of the 31st Division. They attacked on a front of some 1,400 yards. There were twelve Pals Battalions involved which included Accrington, Barnsley, Bradford, Durham, Hull, Leeds and Sheffield.

Their line of attack was to be through Serre with the objective of taking four lines of German trenches before reversing the final line against counter-attack. The story of the attack here was similar to elsewhere on the Somme in as much as the troops were largely mown down by artillery and machine gun fire, either as they climbed out of their trenches or shortly afterwards.

THE BRIGADE COMMANDER – BRIGADIER GENERAL HUBERT REES:

Ten minutes before zero our guns opened an intensive fire. I stood on top to watch it. It was magnificent. The trenches in front of Serre changed shape and dissolved minute by minute under the terrific hail of steel. Watching, I began to believe in the possibility of a great success, but I reckoned without the Hun artillery. As our infantry advanced, down came a perfect wall of explosives along the front trenches. It was the most frightful artillery display that I had seen up to that time, and in some ways, I think it was the heaviest barrage I have seen put down by the defence on any occasion.

The position on the ground for the troops was terrifying. Those who did make the German front line found the wire entanglements largely uncut. They were funnelled into smaller areas where the wire was cut, where they became even more enticing targets. Officers with their distinctive uniforms, Sam Browne belts and in some cases walking sticks or canes, who were generally taller than their men, became specific targets for German marksmen intent on disrupting the chain of command.

PRIVATE GLENN, 12TH BN. YORK AND LANCASTER REGIMENT (SHEFFIELD PALS):

The first line all lay down and I thought they'd had different orders because we had all been told to walk.

It appears that they lay down because they'd been shot and were either dead or wounded. They were just mown down like corn. Our line went forward and the same thing happened. You were just trying to find your way through the shell holes. You could not even see where you were walking!

When we got to the first line of wire, we saw that the first wave were stuck, trying to get through. I didn't get through our wire, and nobody got as far as the German wire.

We weren't getting any orders at all, there was no one left to give any orders, because all the officers had been shot down.

The German artillery, which had not been properly destroyed, was able to bring down accurate fire on the British lines killing those preparing to attack, blocking the trenches with dead and wounded and forcing others out into the open.

PRIVATE PEARSON, 15TH BN. WEST YORKSHIRE REGIMENT (LEEDS PALS):

Every man climbed out of the trenches at the whistle of the officers and not a man hesitated. But I was lucky. I was in part of the trench where the parapet had been battered down as Jerry sought for our trench mortar.

When I ran up the rise out of the trench, I was under a hail of

bullets which were whizzing over my head. Most of our fellows were killed on the parapet.
There was nobody coming forward, the reserves had been shelled in our lines and blown to smithereens. The sergeant decided that as the attack was finished we should go back and try and get into our own lines. We wriggled out of this shell hole and then made a dash!

Because of the purely diversionary nature of the attack at Gommecourt, this attack was in effect the northern end of the anticipated advance. With no attack between them and Gommecourt, and the failure of that attack, the German 66th Regiment immediately to the north were free to subject the Pals to flanking fire.

Although some dispute it, it is claimed that some troops may have actually crossed the first four lines of German trenches and reached as far as Serre itself. If it is true, then they were killed, captured or beaten back without inflicting any significant damage to the enemy or their positions.

Two and a half hours after the start of the attack at 10am that morning, it was all over. Two out of three men who had gone over the top were either dead or wounded on the gentle slope of the ground between the British front line and the German trenches.

However justified or understandable the poor assessment of the strength of the German line and the inadequacies of the British bombardment, there was an example here of inexplicable stupidity.

Before the attack the Royal Engineers had dug five Russian Saps on this Divisional front (there was one at the northern end of the wood as you see it today and one at the southern end with the others fairly evenly spaced over the ground to the south) from the British Front line to within yards of the German line.

These were underground tunnels, known as galleries, which could be used for a number of offensive purposes. These included the insertion of a mine at the Sap head to destroy a section of German trench. Broken through and opened up, the head could equally have provided a pit from which mortars could be fired at close range or a machine gun installed. Alternatively, the openings could have been used as an exit point for grenade carrying troops to bomb their way along the front trench before the Germans had had the opportunity to man the parapet or set up their machine guns.

The Saps covered almost 3,500 yards. They had been authorised by the Army commander, Rawlinson. They had taken five weeks of concentrated effort to excavate, yet not one of them was put to any use whatsoever.

THE CASUALTIES

The Pals Division suffered 3,600 casualties of whom probably about 1,200 were killed.

Although casualties had been expected, mass graves dug and hospital trains laid on, no-one had anticipated the numbers.

PRIVATE PARKER, 12TH BN. YORK AND LANCASTER REGIMENT (SHEFFIELD PALS):

It must have been two or three in the morning before we managed to get the transport and rations up. We had to take the stuff up to Basin Wood, an exposed position about 600 yards behind our front line. It was full of wounded who you could hear groaning and see lying around in the flash of the guns. There were three doctors working flat out but you could see it was a complete shambles.

Serre Cemetery No. 3

I tried to find out about my brother. He'd only come to the Battalion a matter of days before the attack and I had not had enough time to wangle him on to the transport. He had joined C Company but he had not had enough time to pal up with any of them and nobody knew what had happened to him. I never did find out. He must have been blown to smithereens.

Serre Road No. 1 Commonwealth War Grave Cemetery – White Feathers and Boy Soldiers

THE GROUND

Having left your car in front of the cemetery, walk up to the rear left hand side of the cemetery, above the steps and find the grave stone for Horace Iles which is Plot I – E-39.

BOY SOLDIERS

The recruitment of under age boys was not unusual at the beginning of the war. Recruitment offices were faced with tens of thousands of men and youths who were desperate to show their patriotic fervour. To enlist, you had to be eighteen but you could not fight overseas until you were nineteen. Few, if any, of the recruitment officers had the time or inclination to check the age of the volunteers and the attitude of the recruitment sergeants was simple. If a volunteer wanted to fight for his country and was physically fit enough to do so, why stop him? Stories of boys, who declared their real age and were turned away but told to come back the next day when they would be older, were common.

Some boy soldiers were so desperate to join and 'be one of the lads' that they not only lied about their age but also their name. By signing on with a false name, their parents could not track them down and encourage a commanding officer to return their under age son. It is thought that as many as 250,000 boy soldiers were recruited and fought on the front. The youngest is thought to have been Sidney Lewis who was twelve when he enlisted in 1915.

As the war progressed, the issue of boy soldiers became increasingly controversial and was taken up by Sir Arthur Markham, the Liberal MP for Mansfield. Markham used the platform of the House of Commons to

Serre Road Cemetery No. 1

openly question the War Office about its recruitment policy. His principal opponent in this chamber was the Under-Secretary of State for War, Harold Tennant. Within the House, most sided with Tennant as they saw that the well-being of the army was more important than a legal nicety. Markham accused the War Office of deceit. Tennant responded that it was the War Office who had been deceived because it had been the boys who had lied about their age.

As the war proceeded, Markham became inundated with requests from parents who wanted to know where their sons were. Those who had enlisted under false names were all but impossible to contact. Markham concerned himself with those boys aged between fourteen and sixteen. Tennant responded by issuing War Office directives to senior Army officers that boy soldiers should be returned to the UK, but the onus for carrying this through lay with senior army commanders, who were reluctant to lose trained men.

The number of boy soldiers recruited fell drastically after the Battle of the Somme when conscription was brought in and recruits had to provide proof of their age.

WHITE FEATHERS

In August 1914 Admiral Fitzgerald organized a group of 30 women, including several leading female writers of the day, to help 'convince' the men of Britain to join the fight against Germany. Its tactical objective was to shame civilian men into joining the armed services. This aim was to be accomplished by public humiliation, the women handing out white feathers, as a symbol of cowardice, to any man not wearing a uniform. 'The Order of the White Feather' and their recruiting methods quickly spread across Britain.

The youngest soldier killed on 1 July 1916

In some cases it had the desired effect. Sometimes it was given to those who were ineligible to serve or already serving. Siegfried Sassoon was given one on a bus while on leave, when he was in plain clothes. He took it, used it to clean his pipe and then gave it back to the woman!

The impact of white feathers was often tragic, as it was with Horace Iles. Horace was fourteen, but he was big for his age. He worked as a blacksmith's assistant. His size, despite his age, was probably the reason that he was given a white feather when he was travelling home one evening in September 1914 on a tram in Leeds.

Horace Iles.

He was mortified. He came from an Army family, his late father having served as a soldier with Lord Roberts in Afghanistan. Despite the entreaties from his widowed mother and only sister, Florrie, he lied about his age and enlisted.

When Horace Iles arrived in France, he was homesick and wrote to his sister Florrie telling her how unhappy he was. She wrote back saying, "For goodness sake Horace, tell them how old you are. I am sure they will send you back. If you don't do it now you will come back in bits and we want the whole of you!"

Unfortunately, when she wrote the letter Horace had already been killed on the battlefield in front of Serre. Her letter was returned to her, marked 'killed in action.'

At sixteen, Horace Iles was the youngest person to die on 1st July but there were about 500 other boy soldiers who died the same day.

PLACE SIX (Map C, page 150)

Serre Road No. 2 Commonwealth War Grave Cemetery – Wilfred Owen

THE GROUND

Park your car next to the cemetery and then walk up to the stone seat about half way up the cemetery on the eastern, left hand side. This is the approximate position of the German dug-out which the poet Wilfred Owen was ordered to occupy in January 1917.

Serre Road Cemetery No 2 is interesting for a number of reasons. It is considered by many to represent an example of Lutyen's work at its best, with its classical limestone entrance pavilion framing the axis to the stone of Remembrance. The cross is framed by two open pavilions with slightly upswept roofs in a subtle Japanese style.

It was the scene of fierce fighting, attacks and counter-attacks and the ground on which it stands completely fills what was No Man's Land between the British and German lines. It is the largest cemetery on the Somme with over 7,000 graves. They come from all over the battlefield and include every country in the Empire which fought on the Somme and several sets of brothers. Unusually (but like Foncquevillers), it also includes several German graves. (They have a 'roof' profile, rather than the rounded top of the Commonwealth gravestones.)

During the Second World War the war grave' gardener, Ben Leach, stayed behind to tend to the graveyard. When the Germans occupied the area they were impressed and touched by the German graves, and they presented Leach with a bicycle to help him with his work. Leach put it to good use, and in conjunction with his garden shed at the rear of the grave-yard, he was responsible for assisting 32 downed Allied pilots making it safely home to England.

Serre Road Cemetery No. 2 – the diagonal view from the British Front with the cemetery completely filling No Man's Land.

THE ACTION

Owen set off from La Signy Farm, past Basin Wood to the north west, down a communication trench known as Sackville Street, before crossing No Man's Land with about 25 of his men to the position of the old German trenches where there was one of their old dug-outs.

Having been dug by the Germans, the entrance to the dug-out faced the German lines and Owen posted a sentry at the top of the stairs to warn of German attack. They remained in the dug-out for 50 hours during which time they were subjected to a heavy bombardment and the sentry was blown down the steps.

WILFRED OWEN

Wilfred Owen was born in Shropshire in 1893. His father worked on the railways. He attended University College Reading and later taught

English in Bordeaux as a private tutor. He enlisted in 1915, was commissioned into the Manchester Regiment in June 1916 and arrived on the Somme later that year.

During 1917 when he was 24, he was subjected to a number of traumatic experiences. These included being shelled here, falling into a shell hole and suffering concussion, being blown up by a trench mortar and spending several days lying out in No Man's Land amongst what he thought were the remains of a brother officer.

These events caused him to have a nervous breakdown and he was sent to Craiglockhart War Hospital near Edinburgh, where he met Siegfried Sassoon. His doctor encouraged him to write poetry about his experiences. He hesitantly showed his work to Sassoon, of whom he was somewhat in awe. Owen perceived Sassoon was both socially superior as well as being distinguished as a decorated and a well known published poet.

Sassoon, while off-hand with him at their first meeting when Owen came to his room to ask him to autograph a copy of *The Old Huntsman,* was subsequently generous to him, both encouraging him and suggesting changes to his verse.

One of the events Owen recalled and wrote about was the time he spent in this dug-out under enemy fire.

THE SENTRY

We'd found an old Boche dug-out, and he knew,
And gave us hell, for shell on frantic shell
Hammered on top, but never quite burst through.
Rain, guttering down in waterfalls of slime
Kept slush waist high, that rising hour by hour,
Choked up the steps too thick with clay to climb.
What murk of air remained stank old, and sour
With fumes from whizz-bangs, and the smell of men
Who'd lived there years, and left their curse in the den,
If not their corpses...

        There we herded from the blast
Of whizz-bangs, but one found our door at last.
Buffeting eyes and breath, snuffing the candles.
And thud! flump! thud! down the steep steps came thumping

And splashing in the flood, deluging muck –
The sentry's body; then his rifle, handles
Of old Boche bombs, and mud in ruck on ruck.
We dredged him up, for killed, until he whined
"O sir, my eyes – I'm blind – I'm blind, I'm blind!"
Coaxing, I held a flame against his lids
And said if he could see the least blurred light
He was not blind; in time he'd get all right.
"I can't," he sobbed. Eyeballs, huge-bulged like squids
Watch my dreams still; but I forgot him there
In posting next for duty, and sending a scout
To beg a stretcher somewhere, and floundering about
To other posts under the shrieking air.
Those other wretches, how they bled and spewed,
And one who would have drowned himself for good, –
I try not to remember these things now.
Let dread hark back for one word only: how.
Half-listening to that sentry's moans and jumps,
And the wild chattering of his broken teeth,
Renewed most horribly whenever crumps
Pummeled the roof and slogged the air beneath –
Through the dense din, I say, we heard him shout
"I see your lights!" But ours had long died out.

Owen returned to the front in August 1918 but was shot and killed leading an attack in November, seven days before the armistice. He was awarded the Military Cross posthumously. Some consider him the greatest of the First World War poets.

PLACE SEVEN (Location Map only, page 146)

Mailly-Maillet – Shot at Dawn

THE GROUND
Park your car on the side road which is on the north side of the chateau and stand looking at the high wall around the chateau on the road leading into the village.

THE SITUATION IN 1916
Mailly-Maillet was situated two miles behind the British front line. It benefited from extensive underground tunnels, some of which ran for several miles as a result of the historic excavation of building stone. It also had a light railway connecting it to Albert in the south east and Doullens to the north west. For these reasons the village was used constantly throughout the war for billeting troops either on their way up to, or returning from, the front. The remnants of most battalions who were mauled on 1st July around Beaumont-Hamel were withdrawn to this village. At no time was it occupied by the Germans, although it did suffer terrible shell damage.

The village also boasts a church with splendid Gothic carvings on the façade and successful precautions were taken to protect it from enemy shelling. The tower was used as an observation post.

The Café Fly adjacent to the railway station on the north side of the village was utilized as a collecting post for casualties, whilst there was an Advanced Dressing Station in the chateau.

JAMES CROZIER
James Crozier volunteered to join the 9th Royal Irish Rifles on their formation in Belfast in 1914. He was an apprentice in the shipyards. He may have been underage but in any event it was against the wishes of his mother, despite the fact that she accompanied him to the to the recruiting office where she met his future Commanding Officer. He told her not to worry, because he personally would 'keep an eye on her boy.'

The splendid Gothic carvings on the Church of Mailly-Maillet.

He was undersized and once serving, it was evident that he did not have the bearing or temperament of an effective soldier. On 31st January 1916 his battalion entered the front trenches at Serre and at 8.30 that night he was warned off for sentry duty. By 9 o'clock he was 'missing'. Four days later he was apprehended 25 miles behind the lines, without his pay book or any kind of identification, and returned to his unit.

He was court-martialled for desertion. Under the Army Act of the time, judicial execution was justified for ten crimes, one of which was desertion. At his court-martial, Crozier claimed that when he entered the trenches he was both cold and feeling unwell. He said he had pains all over his body. A rifle grenade had fallen within ten yards of him and he had no recollection of either being warned off for duty or leaving the trenches.

The court considered his Army Record. It was poor. He already had two charges for absence. He was found guilty of desertion and sentenced to death. The sentence was ratified by Brigade, Division, Corps and finally by General Haig himself.

The sentence was read out to Rifleman Crozier, and he was publicly drummed out of the service in front of his own battalion before being marched away to await execution, in the detention room in the cellar at 10 Rue Delattre in Auchonvillers, under the custody of the Regimental Police.

His fellow soldiers were very unhappy about the sentence and made their feelings known. The Military Police were worried that there might be a mutiny with the firing squad refusing to shoot. Before being shot, a soldier was entitled to both see a padre and unlimited drink.

At dawn on Sunday 27th February 1916, a firing squad was assembled from his own unit. Crozier was blindfolded, carried out unconscious through drink and tied to a wooden stake in the gardens of the chateau. The battalion was lined up out of sight but within earshot on the adjacent road.

The medical officer pinned a piece of white cloth to the man's tunic as an aiming point and the firing squad fired. Probably out of disgust for the process, most of them shot wide and he was not killed. The firing squad was commanded by a junior officer, perhaps 19 or 20-years-old, known as a subaltern. As previously ordered in this eventuality, the subaltern dispatched Crozier with a single pistol shot to the head at point blank range.

The battalion was marched back to breakfast.

Crozier was cut down and is buried in a marked grave. His gravestone looks no different from any other. The Commanding Officer, who had undertaken to keep an eye on the boy, witnessed the execution. He did, however, try to have Crozier's name included amongst the list of casualties of battle. This would also mean that his mother would receive his death allowance. He was unsuccessful and Rifleman Crozier's mother was notified of the full facts.

THE DEATH SENTENCE

The Duke of Wellington was of the view that, 'punishments are essentially for the sake of example' and in the First World War, one of the factors which was considered by the Commander in Chief before confirming the death sentence, was the perceived discipline in the man's unit.

There was a total of 3,080 death sentences passed between August 1914 and March 1920, of which only 306 were actually carried out. Of these, 291 were serving on the Western Front. The average age of those

The wall of the Chateau Mailly-Maillet.

shot was 25. For the British Army it represented 0.00003% of the 8.9 million troops who served during the war, a minuscule percentage.

65% of the executions were for desertion, which typically ran at over 10% of all men on the Western Front, and, to commanders, a huge, dangerous and worrying statistic. Many men considered imprisonment preferable to service in the trenches and for this reason the use of suspended sentences was encouraged. Of those 306 executed, 91, or about a third, already had suspended sentences and 40 had previously been sentenced to death. (It is perhaps worth considering that during the war in Iraq, almost 3,000 troops went missing from their units between 2003 and 2005.)

With the benefit of medical advances, it is clear that many, but by no means all, of those executed were suffering from some type of mental trauma. Those being tried frequently failed to avail themselves of a defending officer. This meant that there would often be no cross-examination of the prosecuting witness and many of the medical examinations were little more than a cursory formality.

In 1928 the death penalty was abolished for striking a superior officer, disobedience and sleeping at post. The death penalty for cowardice and desertion was finally abolished in 1930.

In 1983 His Honour Judge Babington was permitted to examine all court-martial transcripts on the understanding that he did not record either the unit or the individual's name in his report. His subsequent findings were that in many cases there were legal irregularities and an absence of medical reports, meaning that many of those sentenced to death had not received a fair trial.

In 2005 a Private Members Bill 'Pardon for the soldiers of the Great War,' which named Rifleman Crozier, proposed a tribunal review of all British soldiers sentenced to death. It had the aim, where possible, of recommending a Pardon to the Secretary of State, but failed to make the Statute Book.

In August 2006 the Ministry of Defence finally announced a pardon of all 306 men, including James Crozier.

Mutiny and treason remained capital offences until 1998.

PLACE EIGHT (Map D, page 151)

The Sunken Lane and Malim's Film of the Battle

THE GROUND

There is space to park your car at the end of the lane. On the north side of the main road is a track which cuts through the side of the valley and was known to the troops as the Sunken Lane. At the southern end it is about fifteen feet deep but it rises to the same level as the surrounding ground at the northern end.

It is about 500 yards long with the first 200 yards being below the level of the fields on either side. On the opposite side of the main road and up on the facing valley, slightly to the east, is a clump of trees which marks a spot where there was a German strong-point, known as the Hawthorn Redoubt.

Behind the Sunken Lane, about 200 yards to the west, the plateau fell steeply providing an area of dead ground out of sight to the Germans. This area, which was known as White City, was developed with trenches, dugouts, headquarters, bunkers and first aid posts.

The main road continues to the east into the village of Beaumont-Hamel, which in 1914 had been one of the largest villages on the Somme with over 160 houses.

THE POSITION ON 1ST JULY 1916

Like both Foncquevillers and Mailley-Maillet, the village of Beaumont-Hamel had an extensive system of caves and underground passages on which the Germans capitalised as part of their defensive network.

The line of the German Front had a marked protrusion formed by the Hawthorn Redoubt (on the Hawthorn Ridge). Over the previous seven months, a tunnel had been driven over a distance of 300 yards from behind the British front lines to a position 75 feet under the Redoubt. At the end of the tunnel, a chamber was excavated to hold a 40,600lb charge of ammonal explosive.

The 2nd Royal Fusiliers and four other battalions were to attack towards the Redoubt as soon as the mine was blown and occupy the 'lip' thrown up by the explosion. The 'lip' would act as a dominating feature from which they would then be able to bring down additional fire on the deeper enemy positions in support of the attack.

The 1st Lancashire Fusiliers took up their positions in the Sunken Lane during the night before the attack by approaching along a Russian Sap, or tunnel, which had been dug from the British Front trenches to the rear of the northern end of the lane. The intention was that by using this advanced jumping-off point and not having to negotiate the lane, they would gain precious time in the attack.

The field in front of the Sunken Lane was initially quite flat but about 40 yards further into No Man's Land, there was a sudden drop in the ground, on the far side of which was a very steep bank between three and twelve feet high. This bank, which was to form a deadly hurdle, was completely invisible from the Sunken Lane.

A dispute arose as to the timing of the explosion of the mine. The Corps Commander wanted to blow it at 3.30am in order that the crater could be captured under cover of darkness and consolidated before the attack began. Army Headquarters took the view that such a strategy was unwise because there was a risk that without the final British bombardment immediately before the attack, the Germans would occupy the crater first.

The result was the most unfortunate compromise. It was agreed that the mine should be detonated at 7.20am and, to allow the British to advance, the British artillery were accordingly ordered to lift their bombardment off the German front line ten minutes early. This decision proved to be not only the worst for this particular attack but, it also served to announce the start of the British attack over the entire front.

Geoffrey Malins, the cameraman who was filming the explosion from behind the shoulder of the Sunken Lane (close to Jacob's Ladder), subsequently explained:

The ground gave a mighty convulsion and rocked and swayed. The earth rose in the air to the height of hundreds of feet before with a grinding roar it fell back on itself.

This sequence became the climax of his subsequent film and because it was converted into a postcard and widely sold, it is probably one of the most iconic shots taken in the entire war.

The crater the mine left was 40 feet deep and 130 feet across. The Redoubt was completely destroyed, as were the German garrison and many of the neighbouring trenches and dug-outs. Despite this, the Germans quickly recovered. Free of the British bombardment, they managed to occupy the lip of the crater closest to them before the Royal Fusiliers could arrive in numbers, cutting down the support troops following and calling down their own artillery fire onto the British front line and No Man's Land.

From this position and from the rest of the front line, the Germans were able to put down devastating machine gun fire. Most of the Lancashires were cut down as soon as they left the Sunken Lane and only about 50 got as far as the top of the steep bank where, rather than risk certain suicide, they waited until withdrawing after dark.

It was a sad fate for a battalion which had only the year before fought their way up the beaches and cliffs of Gallipoli, achieving immortal fame by 'winning six VCs before breakfast'.

The mine exploding at Hawthorn Redoubt. Photograph by kind permission and copyright of Imperial War Museums.

The 2nd Royal Fusiliers and the 16th Middlesex (Public Schools Battalion) who were following them suffered a similar fate. As elsewhere on the front, the attack was a complete failure. It was called off at noon and apart from a small holding party, the Sunken Lane was evacuated later that day.

The lane became part of the British front line which became known as Hunter Trench (as shown on Map D) and it was from here that the Argyll and Sutherland Highlanders successfully advanced and captured Beaumont-Hamel as part of the 51st Highland Division on 13th November 1916. The Celtic cross commemorates the Argyll's service on the Somme and the Gaelic inscription translates as 'Friends are good on the day of battle'.

CAMERAMAN GEOFFREY MALINS, JOHN MCDOWELL AND THEIR FILM
Geoffrey Malins started his professional career as a portrait photographer before moving into movies. In November 1915 he went out to France, the War Office having agreed to allow two official cameramen to join the British Expeditionary Force, the equivalent to the 'embedding' of the war correspondents of today.

The unanticipated bank, which had been hidden from view, together with the terrible consequences

By June 1916 he had made 26 films. The work was extremely dangerous and by the end of his first year, he had been wounded twice, deafened, gassed and badly shaken by explosions.

In June 1916 the War Office decided that the forthcoming Somme offensive could be filmed. Malins was joined by a second cameraman called John McDowell. The two men operated in different parts of the British Army's front. Before the battle, Malins had filmed troops on the march and heavy artillery west of Gommecourt, whilst McDowell had filmed pre-battle activities east of Albert. On the opening day of the battle, Malins started on the Sunken Lane, moving later to La Boisselle. McDowell was further south in the vicinity of Carnoy at the start but later he filmed the captured German trenches at Fricourt and Mametz.

On 10th July they both returned to London with some 8,000 feet of film but Malins carried out the editing alone and much of McDowell's film ended up on the cutting room floor.

An image from Geoffrey Malins film 'The Battle of the Somme.'
Photograph by kind permission and copyright Imperial War Museums.

Portrait of J B McDowell, one of the British official cameraman on the Western Front during the First World War, photographed wearing a steel helmet and with a Moy and Bastie cine camera. Photograph by kind permission and copyright of Imperial War Museums.

The completed documentary was first shown in London a month later before going on general release. The film, like most in those days, was both in black and white and silent, but the scenes were interspersed with titles summarising the content. The film was divided into sections with each section showing a phase in the battle from the initial preparations before the attack, through to the attack itself, and finishing with the preparation for further advance. It is thought that a number of the scenes were

The Argyll and Sutherland Highlanders Memorial

actually staged, and in any event the censors undoubtedly played a part in deleting scenes in the film which they considered inappropriate from a morale, strategic or public relations viewpoint.

It was decided that the name of the completed film was to be *The Battle of the Somme.*

The showing of the film was accompanied by a pianist playing a judicious selection from a repertoire of well known popular music. As was the norm, the chosen music would be skilfully synchronised by the pianist to further dramatise the scenes being projected onto the cinema screen.

The film ended up with both documentary and propaganda value because it gave a graphic depiction of trench warfare, including showing dead and wounded British and German soldiers.

The completed film spanned five reels and lasted just over an hour. Its first screening took place to an invited audience in London on 10th August 1916, while the battle still raged. On 21st August the film began showing simultaneously in 34 London cinemas, opening in provincial cities the following week. The Royal family received a private screening at Windsor Castle in September.

For a country which had not been invaded or occupied since 1066, the impact of the film was huge; it was a massive success. Some twenty million tickets were sold in its first six weeks of release, a record not beaten until the arrival of *Star Wars.* It then went on to be distributed in eighteen other countries.

In 1920 Malins published his war memoirs titled *How I Filmed The War.* The book is perhaps most remarkable for the fact that he never once mentions McDowell.

PLACE NINE (Map D, page 151)

Newfoundland Memorial Park – the Newfoundlanders Attack and the Truces the following day

THE GROUND

Park in the car park. The park includes a visitor centre with public conveniences. Climb the Caribou monument which gives an excellent view over the park.

The park covers 84 acres and was purchased by the Government of Newfoundland as a memorial to the soldiers and sailors of Newfoundland who had died in the Great War. It was officially opened by Earl Haig in June 1925. The park stretches from what was a support trench, known as St John's Road, to the German front line trenches at the bottom of the park, known as the Y ravine.

THE SITUATION ON 1ST JULY 1916

The Germans had established a network of deep dug-outs and an underground network of shelters centred on the Y ravine. This deep cutting enabled the Germans to bring reinforcements up to the front under complete cover and the steep banks were tunnelled into to provide shelter for up to a battalion of troops.

As elsewhere on the line, the detonation of the Hawthorn mine just to the north of the park served as a warning to the German troops here that the attack was about to begin.

The Newfoundland Regiment did not receive their orders to begin their attack until 8.45am by which time the earlier waves of troops had failed to achieve their objectives.

They moved off half an hour later in their predetermined sections of ten men, with 25 paces between sections and 100 yards between companies. As soon as they left St John's Road and Clonmel Avenue, they were visible and subjected to both artillery fire and machine gun fire from their front, the Y ravine to their flank, and the high ground further east.

Their contemporaneous War Diary states:

> *The enemy's fire was effective from the outset but the heaviest casualties occurred on passing through the gaps in our own wire where the men were mown down in heaps. Many more gaps in the wire were required than had been cut. In spite of losses the survivors steadily advanced until close to the enemy's wire by which time very few remained although a few men are believed to have actually succeeded in throwing bombs into the enemy trenches.*

At 9.45am their Commanding Officer reported personally to Brigade Battle Headquarters that the attack had failed. During the evening and night, unwounded survivors managed to crawl back to their own lines and by next morning 68 had answered their names.

In addition to the 77 killed and 23 who died of their wounds, 374 were wounded and 210 were missing, believed dead. Tragically five members of the Ayre family were to die that day, four of whom were serving with the Newfoundlanders.

An old shell hole filled with water.

The lines of the old trenches.

2ND JULY 1916 AND SUBSEQUENT TRUCES

The morning after the Big Push where the attack had failed, unofficial truces broke out. A German medical officer approached the British trenches at Gommecourt to arrange an armistice and the Germans then let British troops move freely in front of their trenches to recover their wounded.

Around the Hawthorn mine, the Germans collected British wounded, having come out of their trenches under cover of a Red Cross flag.

In front of Beaumont-Hamel, a young soldier from the Worcesters, who had crawled out, concealed by the morning mist to search for a wounded comrade, had miraculously found him close to the German wire but was seen by the Germans when the mist suddenly cleared.

There was a clatter of rifle bolts but as both British soldiers looked up, a sharp order was given and a German officer sprang on to the parapet of the enemy trench. He shouted across in surprisingly good English, "You must not stop there with that man. If you want to come in, come along, otherwise you must go back to your own trenches." And he added as the boy hesitated, "We will look after your comrade."

"I'll go back to my own trenches sir," he shouted back before crawling back to his own lines through the shell holes and bodies; no one fired at his retreating back.

On 4th July there was a more formal truce when officers from both sides advanced under Red Cross flags into No Man's Land. They stopped once they had both progressed as far as they felt appropriate, saluted and then supervised stretcher parties to recover as many of the wounded as were still alive and many of the dead. Not a word was spoken between the two sides and after a long afternoon, the two officers again saluted before returning to their own trenches.

PLACE TEN (Map D, page 151)

51st Highland Division Memorial: Second Battle of Beaumont-Hamel

13-19th November 1916.

THE GROUND

Walk down to the memorial of the Highland soldier which stands at the head of the Y ravine.

The cemetery behind you (which follows the circular line of the original shell hole) stands on the German front line. The wire in front of it was different to the extent that it was supplemented by a single strand of wire placed just above ground level in front of the main entanglement to act as a trip wire. Behind this wire the Germans had sunk spikes which protruded about a foot above ground level and were intended to transfix any man who tripped and fell onto them.

THE SECOND BATTLE

High Command never gave up hope of launching a second successful attack on Beaumont-Hamel. Preparations were made and a new mine was inserted under Hawthorn close to the original. Jumping-off trenches were dug closer to the German front and on 11th November tanks moved up to White City in preparation for the offensive.

The attack was made by the Highland Division, consisting of kilted Highland regiments. There was tremendous Divisional pride, even though individual battalions were frequently in fights with each other. As a Division they considered both that they were elite and that they were specifically reserved for hard battles.

The attack began at 5.45am on 13th November with the detonation of the Hawthorn mine in thick fog, but with a concentration of artillery on the objectives which was greater than had been allocated to the entire front on 1st July. Although the British barrage moved too far ahead of the

A Highlander of the 51st Division overlooking the Y Ravine.

attacking troops, the Seaforth Highlanders managed to fight through Beaumont-Hamel, consolidate their final objective, take 600 prisoners and over the following two days repel several enemy counter-attacks.

To their south, the Argyll and Sutherland Highlanders, despite losses from machine gun fire, also took their objectives, securing the flank to the Seaforths and clearing the dug-outs and cellars in the village. The tanks approached from White City but became bogged down in No Man's Land.

The Black Watch and the Gordon Highlanders were successful in taking the Y ravine, assisted by the weight of the bombardment, the fog and the fact that the Germans realised Beaumont-Hamel village had already fallen.

It is perhaps this action, more than any other, and the taking of a position which the enemy considered impregnable, that caused the Germans to christen the kilted highlanders, "the ladies from Hell".

2LT NORMAN COLLINS – 1/6TH SEAFORTH HIGHLANDERS, AGED 19

When war was declared, Norman Collins was seventeen, living with his parents in Hartlepool and working as an apprentice in the drawing office of a shipping company building ships for the Royal Navy.

He enlisted on the first day of the war but his father intercepted him at the railway station, and together with a director from the shipping company, explained to the recruiting officer that not only was he involved in war work but he was also under age.

As soon as he was eighteen, he capitalised on the fact that free railway tickets were available for potential recruits to travel to the Regimental depot of their choice. Knowing that the Seaforth Highlanders had a depot at Dingwall, north of Inverness, making it more difficult for his parents to find him and bring him home, and believing that the Seaforths were considered a good regiment with whom he was likely to see some fighting, he took the train to Dingwall and enlisted.

Collins had always been interested in the army and had joined the cadet force at school. He was dedicated, diligent and ambitious. He worked his way through the junior ranks and was selected to take the necessary exams to secure a commission as an officer. Through hard work and application he passed the exams and was commissioned into the Seaforths.

He arrived in France in time for the attack on Beaumont-Hamel.

Everyone went in with fixed bayonets and as many mills bombs as they could carry. The officers carried a cane, a walking stick, a revolver and a few bombs. The cane was no use whatever and the stick was just a bit of show!

At 5.45 it was still dark and there was thick fog, then suddenly a mine went up (at Hawthorn) and 2,000 guns opened fire on their trenches. The whole horizon seemed to go up in flames. It was so loud you couldn't pick out individual shells; it was just a continuous drumming.

Then there was dead silence and the sudden contrast was stunning. About two minutes later our artillery, having raised their sights, dished out a further barrage on their second line. Every minute a shell fell on every yard of their ground.

I suppose I might have blown a whistle to get the jocks moving but it didn't mean anything, so you sort of shepherded the men over. You are very aware of the example you are setting the men; if they saw you flunking it, showing fear, they wouldn't think much of you.

As we went forward I saw men dropping all around me. I noticed a

Wrapped in Army blankets they were buried side by side like sardines.

Gordon Highlander pitch forward onto his hands and knees. I went up to him and he was stone dead, his kilt raised showing his back side. Had he been wounded I would not have had time to stop.

The Germans were taken entirely by surprise and their front line was captured fairly easily with few losses. The bombardment had cut quite a bit of their defensive wire and their trenches were just wiped out. It was only by the mouths of the dugouts that one could tell that there had been a trench.

I wasn't in the first wave which captured the front line; we advanced through the first wave and went on under a canopy of steel to their second and third lines. The Germans managed to get their machine guns up and they opened fire on us. I must say this, the Germans were good soldiers. Many fought to the end and I saw one machine gun post fight to their last bullet. I really admired them as soldiers.

My role was to get into their trenches and throw mills bombs down into their dugouts saying "Share that amongst you!"

We took several hundred prisoners. There was nothing left of the village of Beaumont-Hamel. It had been so badly pulverised by shelling that it could only be identified by a map reference.

A day or two afterwards I had a good look around the German dugouts in Y Ravine. They were very deep and had flights of stairs down to the bottom. There were wire beds and a system of brass bells which a batman could ring before entry into the officers' quarters. They were such a contrast to our own trenches.

Sometime later I was appointed burial officer with the task of burying the dead. I had a squad of men to help me with picks and shovels and also stretchers. In a Highland Regiment many of the men are from the same family. Some of the men we were picking up were their brothers or cousins and they were upset, very, very upset.

We took our own dead back to Mailly-Maillet Wood on stretchers. We dug a long trench and put the dead in there, wrapped in army blankets, neatly packed like sardines. They fell side by side and we buried them side by side. I think there were about 80 of them.

I thought we were finished but afterwards I was ordered back under shell fire into what had been No Man's Land to bury the old dead of the Newfoundland Regiment killed on 1st July.

A few of my party were knocked out by shell fire and we had some *miraculous escapes. A six inch shell burst about ten yards away from me but I was only covered in mud.*

The flesh had mainly gone from their faces but the hair and beard had grown to some extent. When you touched a body, rats ran out of the chest cage. We left the identity disc on the bodies so that they could be identified later but removed their pay books inside which was photographs of their mothers and fathers, sweethearts and children as well as their last will and testament. We put all these personal items in a clean sandbag then we shovelled the dead into shell holes, about 30 at a time and covered them up as best we could.

It was the most loathsome job I've ever had.

*The cemetery follows the line of the shell hole in which the bodies
were buried*

PLACE ELEVEN (Map E, page 152)

The Ulster Tower Memorial and the Ulster Volunteer Force

THE GROUND

There is a small parking area in front of the tower and a café and public conveniences at the rear.

The memorial is a replica of a tower known as Helen's Tower on the Marquis of Dufferin and Ava's estate at Clandeboye in County Down, north east of Belfast in Northern Ireland where the 36th (Ulster) Division trained before coming to France. It was built in 1921 to commemorate the Ulster Division's involvement in the battle. It stands 100 yards in front of the German trench line facing Thiepval Wood, the front edge of which was held by the Ulster Division on the other side of the road known as Mill Road. A short distance to the west of the tower is a spot where the remnants of a German machine gun post can still be seen (11a on Map E).

BACKGROUND TO THE ULSTER DIVISION

When war broke out, the Ulster Volunteer Force (UVF) was 80,000 strong, well armed and well drilled. It was the Ulster Protestant force formed in response to the threat of Home Rule for the majority Catholic south. Kitchener reached an agreement with Sir Edward Carson, the Unionist leader, that on the basis that the British Government would put the entire question of Home Rule to one side for the duration of the war, the UVF would be incorporated into the British Army. Many of the battalions were firmly based on their UVF origins and the Divisional sign was the Red Hand of Ulster.

ACTION ON 1ST JULY 1916

The first VC of the day was awarded posthumously to Rifleman Billy McFadzean of the Royal Irish Rifles in Thiepval Wood. Billy was 21 years old and a keen rugby player, weighing over 13 stone, and had also been an enthusiastic member of the UVF in Belfast. Early that morning he was carrying a box of grenades to the front in Elgin Avenue for distribution when it slid out of his grip into the trench and the safety pins of two of the bombs fell out. He heard the pop of an igniter cap and knowing that there would shortly be an explosion, lethal in a packed communication trench, he flung himself on top of the box to absorb the blast and spare his comrades.

The Ulster Division objective was to attack over Mill Road through a strong point, which was known as the Schwaben Redoubt (behind and to the north east of the tower), and then on to the second and third German lines beyond.

The Ulstermen had dug shallow trenches out into No Man's Land towards Mill Road and Thiepval Road before the attack. On the day, encouraged by the choice of date for the attack, which commemorated the Battle of the Boyne in the old Gregorian Calendar, and fortified with drink, they attacked at the run, under cover of a smoke screen and before the artillery bombardment had lifted. They took the first German line, sending back 500 prisoners. They then continued to a distance of almost

Mill Road which was heaped with dead and dying.

The Ulster Tower seen from Mill Road Cemetery.

a mile. It was the only place north of the Albert to Bapaume road where the German lines were seriously penetrated.

However, the German artillery made it impossible for them to be supported by later attacks. They were exposed on their flanks where the attack had failed and they were subjected to fierce counter-attacks. No Man's Land, over which they had so wisely and quickly run, was traversed by machine gun fire from the Thiepval Fort, a strong point to the north of the old chateau which dominated the entire area.

After fourteen hours, those that could were forced to withdraw. Most, however, had made their last move. The conditions were indescribably bad with the dead lying in heaps. Casualties were so appalling that the medical staff were unable to cope, with fresh cases arriving before the earlier ones could be attended to or evacuated. The tracks to the rear became choked with walking wounded and ambulances and Mill Road was heaped high with corpses.

When relief troops came up that evening, they heard not only the roar of explosions but a different sound that none of them had ever heard before. It was a sound which raised the hair on the backs of their necks and was a sound which they prayed they would never hear again. It was the sound of the wounded lying out in No Man's Land. Some were screaming with pain, some were shouting for help or groaning in delirium, while others were weeping more quietly. As the gunfire died down and the dawn of a new day broke, this other sound filled the air.

The Pope's Nose and the Maxim Machine Gun

THE GROUND

The tip of the German salient was known to the British as the Pope's Nose and in a wonderful commanding position are the concrete remains of a German machine gun post. It is worth visiting if only to contemplate both the development of this machine and its killing power in terms of rate of fire and range.

The remains of the machine gun post at the Pope's Nose.

SIR HIRAM STEVENS MAXIM (1840-1916)

Maxim was American born but moved to Great Britain where he designed an automatic weapon which utilized the natural recoil of the first shot to eject the spent cartridge and compress a spring to prepare the gun for the second. The gun was more efficient and reliable than any earlier such machines and was put into commercial production with the financial support of Edward Vickers. The design was improved and developed into the Maxim-Vickers Machine Gun.

The gun was first demonstrated in 1884, and first issued to British Colonial Forces for the Matabele War in Rhodesia. Thereafter it was to play an important part in the colonization of Africa. It was adopted by the British Army before the First World War and similar variations based on the same design were used by both the Russian and German Forces.

It was belt fed, water-cooled and could fire initially around 400, but eventually up to 600, rounds a minute. Although it was typically used at ranges of up to 1,500 yards, the bullets could be made to fall up to 3,500 yards away (two miles). It was heavy and cumbersome (it required a team of eight men) and it stood on a tripod, which gave it the advantage that it could be sighted in daylight and then fired on a fixed line in darkness or through smoke.

The British were initially slow to appreciate the potential of this fearsome machine, while the Germans fully exploited its capability into their defensive network from the outset of the war. In time, the British became adept in the use of machine gun fire not only for defence, shooting directly at the attacking forces, but also indirectly, in support of attacks, by firing at an angle over the heads of their own advancing infantry with the cone, or beaten zone, of the bullets being used to supplement artillery fire.

PLACE TWELVE (Map E, page 152)

Thiepval Memorial to the Missing

THE GROUND

There is a large car park by the Thiepval Visitors Centre. The centre has a cinema showing films of the war, a shop and public conveniences.

THE MEMORIAL

Thiepval is the largest Commonwealth war memorial in the world. It stands 140 feet high, dominating the battlefield, and sits on a concrete raft nineteen feet thick which bridges the tunnels and dug-outs of the old German position. It is a massive red brick tower penetrated by arches supported by sixteen wide brick pillars clad with Portland stone, which provide enough wall space for the inscription of all the names of soldiers with no known graves. It is considered by some to be the greatest piece of British architecture of the 20th century. On the far side are 600 graves of which 300 are Empire Troops and 300 French.

The Lutyens' Thiepval Memorial to the missing which dominates the battlefield.

Many of the soldiers left letters to be sent on to their loved ones in the event of their death:

ACTING CAPTAIN LEN HAVILLAND LE MESURIER, KINGS ROYAL RIFLE CORPS – aged 22, a scholar from University College, Oxford.

Dearest Mother,
I am writing this because the battalion is going into action tomorrow and I shall leave it with instructions that it shall be sent on to you if I am killed. I am doing so because I think you will like it, even if it revives your grief for a short time.
If the worst should happen I want you to try and see things like this. Tomorrow I know I shall have to face the most terrible and degrading sensation that we all have to face, the fear of death, and I know that I shall fear and hate the prospect of it as everybody does.
Above all I hate the idea of dying before my life has really begun and before I have had the chance to make a success or failure of it. But I also want you to realize that if I do fall, that death in action tomorrow is the finest death that could come to any man and I shall be proud to have died for my country.

I know in your brave moments what you wish and expect of me. My only prayer is that you too will be proud and not too sorry that I have met my fate.
Goodbye. Much love and many kisses, Len

Len's name is inscribed on Pillar Face 13 of the Thiepval memorial. The memorial has over 72,000 other names of soldiers whose bodies, like Len's, were never found.

Names of the missing carved into the pillars and stretching out of sight

GEOFFREY ANKETELL STUDDERT KENNEDY, MC (27TH JUNE 1883-8TH MARCH 1929)

Kennedy was the seventh of nine children and was born in Leeds. His father was a vicar. He was educated at the local grammar school and Trinity College, Dublin, following which he entered the church and subsequently became the vicar of St Paul's in Worcester.

On the outbreak of World War I, Kennedy volunteered as a chaplain and by December 1915 he was in France. He was a great communicator and could pack a hall using jokes, self deprecation, powerful sermons and community singing. Men would queue up waiting for him to read or write letters home for them. He gained the nickname 'Woodbine Willie' as a result of his habit of giving away cigarettes to the troops in vast quantities.

When Revd. Theodore Hardy (Place 3) first arrived in France, he sought out Kennedy, who was twenty years his younger, for advice. The advice he got was to live with the men, go where they went and share the same risks. He was told by Kennedy that the best place for a padre was where there was the most danger of death.

Kennedy was hugely impressed by Hardy's quiet humility and never forgot his one meeting. In 1917, Kennedy won the Military Cross at Messines Ridge and, like Hardy, was appointed Chaplain to the King.

He wrote a number of poems about his experiences, and these appeared in the books *Rough Rhymes of a Padre* (1918), and *More Rough Rhymes* (1919). The two poems below both appear in the first book. Both are relevant to Thiepval.

HIS MATE

There's a broken, battered village
Somewhere up behind the line,
There's a dug-out and a bunk there
That I used to say were mine.

I remember how I reached them,
Dripping wet and all forlorn,
In the dim and dreary twilight
Of a weeping summer morn.

All that week I'd buried brothers,
In one bitter battle slain,
In one grave I laid two hundred.
God! What sorrow and what rain!

And that night I'd been in trenches,
Seeking out the sodden dead,
And just dropping them in shell-holes,
With a service swiftly said.

For the bullets rattled round me,
But I couldn't leave them there,
Water-soaked in flooded shell-holes,
Reft of common Christian prayer.

So I crawled round on my belly,
And I listened to the roar
Of the guns that hammered Thiepval,
Like big breakers on the shore.

Then there spoke a dripping sergeant,
When the time was growing late,
"Would you please to bury this one,
'Cause e' used to be my mate?"

So we groped our way in darkness
To a body lying there,
Just a blacker lump of blackness,
With a red blotch on his hair.

Though we turned him gently over,
Yet I still can hear the thud,
As the body fell face forward,
And then settled in the mud.

We went down upon our faces,
And I said the service through,
From 'I am the Resurrection'
To the last, the great 'adieu.'

We stood up to give the Blessing,
    And commend him to the Lord,
When a sudden light shot soaring
    Silver swift and like a sword.

At a stroke it slew the darkness,
    Flashed its glory on the mud,
And I saw the sergeant staring
    At a crimson clot of blood.

There are many kinds of sorrow
    In this world of Love and Hate,
But there is no sterner sorrow
    Than a soldier's for his mate.

I Know Not Where They Have Laid Him

I wouldn't mind if I only knowed
The spot where they'd laid my lad;
If I could see where they'd buried 'im,
It wouldn't be arf so bad.
But they do say some's not buried at all,
Left to the maggots and flies,
Rottin' out there in that No Man's Land,
Just where they falls — they lies.
Parson 'e says as it makes no odds,
'Cause the soul o' the lad goes on,
'Is spirit 'as gorn to 'is Gawd, 'e says,
Wherever 'is body 'as gorn.
But Parson ain't never 'ad no child,
'E's a man, not a woman, see?
'Ow can he know what a woman feels,
And what it can mean to me?
For my boy's body were mine — my own,
I bore it in bitter pain,
Bone of my bone and flesh of my flesh,
It lies and rots in the rain.
Parson ain't never suckled a child
Nor broken 'is nights o' rest,

To 'ush it to sleep in 'is aching arms,
While it drew life from 'is breast.
'E ain't never watched by a sick child's bed
Nor seed it fightin' for life,
A man don't know what a mother knows,
'E leaves all that to 'is wife.
I minds that chapter as Parson read
When poor little Jenny died,
And I were feeling as I feel now,
Wiv this emptiness inside.
Thou Fool — it said — thou Fool — for to ask
And 'ow do the dead arise?
What is the body that they shall wear
Up there in God's Paradise?
I may be a fool, but that's just it,
That's just what I wants to know,
What is the body my boy shall bear,
And 'ow does that body grow?
I reckons as 'ow that Scripture piece
Were writ by a single man,
They never knows what a body costs
And I don't see 'ow they can.
A married man 'as a bit ov sense
If 'e's been and stood wiv 'is wife,
'E knows the body 'is baby wears
'As cost 'er all but 'er life.

But even a Father never knows
The ache in a Mother's 'eart,
When she and the body 'er body bore
Are severed and torn apart.
The men wouldn't make these cursed wars
If they knowed of a body's worth,
They wouldn't be blowin' 'em all to bits
If they 'ad the pains ov birth.
But bless ye — the men don't know they're born,
For they gets away scot free.

'Ow can they know what their cruel wars
Is costin' the likes ov me?
I were proud to give, I'd give again
If I knowed the cause were right,
For I wouldn't keep no son of mine
When 'is dooty called to fight.
But I'd like to know just where it's laid,
That body my body bore,
And I'd like to know who'll mother 'im
Out there on that other shore,
Who will be bearin' the mother's part
And be makin' your body, boy?
Who will be 'avin' the mother's pain,
And feelin' the mother's joy?

Gawd, is it you? Then bow you down
And 'ark to a Mother's prayer.
Don't keep it all to yourself, Good Lord,
But give 'is old Mother a share.
Gimme a share of the travail pain
Of my own son's second birth,
Double the pain if you double the joy
That a mother feels on earth.
Gimme the sorrow and not the joy
If that 'as to be your will,
Gimme the labour and not the pride,
But make me 'is mother still.
Maybe the body as 'e shall wear
Is born of my breaking heart,
Maybe these pains are the new birth pangs
What'll give my laddie 'is start.
Then I'd not trouble 'ow hard they was,
I'd gladly go through the mill,
If that noo body 'e wore were mine,
And I were 'is mother still.

PLACE THIRTEEN (Map F, page 153)

Lochnagar Crater and the Capture of La Boisselle

THE GROUND

There is a rough car parking area adjacent to the mine.

No Man's Land was probably narrower at the small village of La Boisselle than anywhere else along the Somme front. The lines came to within less than fifteen yards of each other and this had resulted in extensive mining by both sides. The area of the Glory Hole still shows the results.

The village occupies a spur of high ground, either side of which are two valleys known to the British as Sausage on the south side and Mash on the north.

In order to facilitate the attack, two mines were to be detonated, one just to the north of the village known as the Y Sap mine and this one, which is 50% larger, further south under the German Schwaben Höhe Redoubt, which dominated the ground over a wide area.

The objective of a mine was typically three-fold: first, to destroy an enemy position with the associated damage to dug-outs, trenches and the morale of the local defenders; second, to throw up a lip around the mine which could be used by the attackers as a defensive and offensive feature behind which they could take shelter, and finally to create a physical obstacle to reduce any flanking or enfilade fire.

The mine crater is named after a British communication trench called Lochnagar Street, which was where the tunnel began. Lochnagar is a loch in the centre of the Royal family's Balmoral Estate in Aberdeenshire. The communication trench was almost certainly named by the Gordon Highlanders, who recruited from Aberdeenshire, when they took over the area from the French in 1915.

THE SITUATION ON 1ST JULY 1916

This sector was attacked by the 34th (Tyneside) Division which was entirely made up of New Army soldiers. The initial aim was to attack either side, leaving the village to be taken subsequently by bombing parties.

Lochnagar was dug by 179th Tunneling Company and packed with two explosive charges totaling 26.8 tons. It was exploded with sixteen other mines at 7.28am and left a crater measuring 300 feet across and 90 feet deep. Although the 'lip' around this crater has been removed, the hole itself is still awe inspiring.

The sound of the explosion was heard in Downing Street and the shockwaves through the ground were such that a soldier, who was sitting with his legs braced across a trench at the time of detonation, had them broken.

CECIL LEWIS OF THE RFC:

At La Boisselle the earth heaved and flashed, a tremendous and magnificent column rose up into the sky. There was an air splitting roar, drowning all the guns, flinging my aircraft sideways in the repercussion air. The earthly column rose, higher and higher to almost four thousand feet. There it hung or seemed to hang, for a moment in the air, like the silhouette of some great cypress tree, then fell away in a widening cone of dust and debris.

As it settled, the Tyneside began their attack. The smaller mine on the north of village caused no casualties as the troops had been withdrawn but the Lochnagar mine was effective and resulted in debris falling on the entire Baden Regiment for over a minute. The surviving Badeners silently held their fire until the first wave of troops reached the lip of the mine. Then there was a hurricane of fire.

PRIVATE ROY BEALING, MM, THE WILTSHIRE REGIMENT:

When the whistle went, I threw my rifle on the top of the trench and clambered out of it, grabbed the rifle and started going forward. There were shell holes everywhere. I had not gone far before I fell in one. There were so many shell holes you could not get around them. But you had to go on so, every time I stumbled and fell in a shell hole, I just waited a quarter of a minute, had another breath, and then out of it and on again.

I must have fallen half a dozen times before I got to the front line, and there were lads falling all over the place. You didn't know whether they were just tripping over like me, or whether they were going down with bullets in them, because it wasn't just the shells exploding round about, it was the machine guns hammering out like hell from the third German line because it was on slightly higher

ground. Lucas went down. I'd had to help him fix his bayonet he had been shaking so badly before the attack. He was killed before he even got to the first trench, the one which was already partly in our hands.

I got to the parapet, it looked just like a parapet, and chalk banked up, and flung myself over it. Well then, I didn't know where I was! I went straight down sixty feet or more, sliding and slithering. I thought I'd never come to the bottom! Of course it was the big crater where they had blown the mine. There were half a dozen of us all rattling down, shouting. We picked ourselves up and Captain Lefroy was there and Sergeant Stone and just about fourteen or fifteen of us, out of the whole company. Captain Lefroy got us together and we clambered up the opposite side of the crater and lay there, well under cover, half way up and looking around to see if any more was coming in. We had two brothers named Moxham and one of them was with us and, looking across, we see his brother coming on the opposite lip of the crater. He stopped and didn't throw himself over it like we had, unexpected like, he just stood there looking down into it. We all shouted, "Come on, come on! Don't stand there! That bloomin' machine gun'll come round. He'll catch you!" But he just stood there a moment too long and it did get him! He was killed outright. Of course his brother didn't know what to do with himself.

A while after another chap called Bill Parratt came over and he was getting down the crater, careful like, when a shell dropped right beside him. There was a big cloud of smoke and when it cleared we saw it had dropped him right at the bottom of the crater. He was lying on his back, one of his legs had been blown off and it was two or three yards from him. He was hurt bad. He must have been in pain and agony, but there was nothing we could do for him. As the day went on, and it got towards evening, he started to cry out, "Captain Lefroy, come and shoot me." He kept calling out over and over again, "Captain Lefroy come and shoot me." We got fed up with hearing him calling out.

Makes you jangly, all this calling, "come and shoot me, come and shoot me." So the Captain crawls down and went over to him and pulled a packet out of his pocket and it was morphia tablets. He knew he couldn't do anything for him, just give him these tablets, and he got them down Bill and after a bit he went quiet and gradually faded out.

The trees and bushes around the crater give some idea of what the lip would have looked like after the explosion.

Although the number of troops was small, some managed to advance both north and south of the crater. To the south east of the Schwaben Höhe were two further redoubts known as Sausage and Scots. The 11th Suffolks tried to fight their way through the Sausage Redoubt only to be burnt to death by German flamethrowers as they reached the parapets. Scots was briefly captured but a second assault on Sausage was again unsuccessful and this position, together with the un-captured La Boisselle, came under fire from a German field howitzer battery at Ponziers, which inflicted further terrible casualties on the attacking troops.

Despite this, some troops managed to penetrate as far as Contalmaison but they were exposed on their flanks and could not be supported by subsequent troops. Subjected to effective counter-attacks, like elsewhere, they were forced to withdraw.

The crater remained in British hands, the tunnel was reopened allowing troops safe access and further attacks were mounted on 2nd and 3rd July, ultimately being successful under the leadership of one-eyed, one-armed Lieutenant Colonel Carton De Wiart of the 8th Gloucesters.

The Somme Battlefield

CARTON DE WIART

Carton De Wiart was the most extraordinary man. His father was Belgian, his mother Irish. He was a born soldier. Studying at Balliol, Oxford, when the Boer War broke out, he enlisted as a trooper with a yeomanry regiment without his father's consent. He was twice wounded and invalided back home. His father relented, allowed him to leave Oxford and secure a commission with the Dragoon Guards. He served in Somaliland with the Camel Corps and added to his injuries by losing an eye fighting the Dervishes. On recovery, and having passed the medical board on condition he wore a glass eye, he arrived in France in time to lose his hand at Ypres. Back at the front in 1916, having demonstrated to the medical board his dexterity with his remaining hand, he was given command of 8th Gloucesters and ordered to try and capture La Boisselle, the attacks on 1st and 2nd July having failed.

We moved up on the night of the 2nd July to attack the next morning. The spirit of the men was amazing, for although they knew that they were going to have a bad time and that casualties would be heavy, they seemed not to have a care in the world.

No Man's Land presented a ghastly sight for it was strewn with British corpses in those grotesque attitudes particular to the dead on a battlefield.

A battalion commander has no time to sit around in the dug-out provided for him. My battalion were untried troops and an invisible commander cannot be a great source of inspiration to get them out of their trenches, advance over blown up wire and piled up corpses and pitch themselves into battle.

We were the support battalion and as we advanced the lead battalion ahead of us came under a heavy German barrage and in the noise and confusion they began to retire through my men.

Retirement is the most infectious disease and there was a desperate moment of chaos, when the issue hung in the balance. The officers of the 8th Gloucesters were truly magnificent, and the men rallied and responded to them. They advanced regardless of their appalling casualties until they had fulfilled their appointed task and captured La Boisselle.

During that engagement I was compelled to use some bombs for the first and last time, and with only one arm to throw with, I found a new use for my teeth, pulling the pins out; I was thankful that my teeth were my own.

In his book *Happy Odyssey*, Carton De Wiart explains that the hospital on Park Lane, London, kept his silk pyjamas in readiness for his next visit but never mentions that he was awarded a VC for his part in capturing La Boisselle.

The citation reads:

For most conspicuous bravery, coolness and determination during severe operations of a prolonged nature. It was owing, in great measure, to his dauntless courage and inspiring example that a serious reverse was averted. He displayed the utmost energy and courage in forcing our attack home. After three other battalion commanders had become casualties, he controlled their commands, and ensured that the ground won was maintained at all costs. He frequently exposed himself in the organization of positions and supplies, passing unflinchingly through fire barrage of the most intensive nature. His gallantry was inspiring to all.

MAJOR JOHN NORTON-GRIFFITHS MP, FOUNDER OF THE ROYAL ENGINEERS TUNNELLING COMPANIES

Norton-Griffiths was yet another extraordinary man. Born in Somerset, the son of the Clerk of the Works for the local estate, he left home at seventeen and joined the Life Guards as a trooper. On the outbreak of the Second Matabele War in 1886, he enlisted as a sergeant with the British South African Police and by the end of the Second Boer War, he had become Captain Adjutant to Lord Roberts' bodyguard.

After the Boer War, he set up an engineering company and proceeded to win lucrative contracts to carry out major engineering projects in both Africa and South America. He became comfortably wealthy and in 1910 was elected to Parliament as the Conservative member for Wednesbury in Staffordshire.

His engineering company continued to flourish and he secured contracts for sewerage pipes in Liverpool and Manchester. Relatively small-bore tunnels were required which were being bored by a manual technique known as 'clay-kicking.' The man doing the digging sat with his back to a wooden frame facing the end of the tunnel. He could then use his feet to kick a spade-like implement into the clay, passing the spoil over his shoulder to his mate for disposal.

At the start of the war in 1914 Norton-Griffiths, fiercely patriotic, raised the 2nd King Edward's Horse at his own expense and was commissioned as a Major into the regiment. In early December 1914, he wrote to the War Office suggesting that 'clay-kicking' would be a useful technique to assist both attacking, spying and intercepting German tunnels coming in the opposite direction. His letter was filed.

Later that month the Germans dug shallow tunnels through No Man's Land at Givenchy and blew eight 50 kilogram (110lb) mines, which they co-ordinated with a successful infantry attack, leading to the loss of an entire company of 800 Empire troops.

Norton-Griffiths's letter was retrieved from filing and a telegram was sent ordering him to report to Lord Kitchener in the War Office. Immediately on arrival, he took a coal shovel from the fire grate and sitting on the floor, gave a demonstration of 'clay-kicking.' Impressed but sceptical, Kitchener ordered Norton-Griffiths to travel straight to France, explain his method to the commanders and to investigate the suitability of the Flanders soil for the process.

Skilled at public relations, securing contracts and something of a show-man, Norton-Griffiths demonstrated his method to the Engineer-in-Chief, as well as at headquarters at all levels – Brigade, Division, Corps and Army. He was also able to confirm the excellent texture of the clay-based soil.

It was agreed that Tunnelling Companies would be formed within the Royal Engineers which, in order to ensure the minimum of delay, would be manned by the recruitment of civilian miners who would be paid six shillings a day, twice that of ordinary miners and six times more than ordinary soldiers.

On this decision Norton-Griffiths terminated one of his Liverpool tunnelling contracts and made eighteen of his staff redundant. The following day the eighteen Liverpool men turned up in Chatham to be enrolled into the Royal Engineers as sappers. Four days later these very same men were working underground on the Western Front.

'Clay-kicking' gave the British tunnellers two advantages over their German counterparts. In contrast to the Germans who used pick-axes and other noise making tools, which made tunnels more vulnerable to detection and attack, 'clay-kicking' was a virtually silent method of tunnelling. Its other advantage was that it was up to four times faster than the German system. British tunnels could progress at up to 25 feet in a day.

It was evident that huge numbers of miners would be required. Norton-Griffiths used his skills as a politician and as an engineer and his strength of character to persuade commanding officers to release men he believed to be ideally suited to mining (generally those men who had worked as miners before war broke out). He also took pains to integrate these civilians into the military environment. He became a familiar sight, touring the British lines in his battered Rolls Royce loaded with crates of fine wine.

Norton-Griffiths was promoted to Colonel and awarded the DSO. After the war he was created a baronet and died in 1930 just after becoming grandfather to Jeremy Thorpe, the future leader of the Liberal party.

One of the few remaining post-war timber houses built for the returning residents at La Boisselle.

PLACE FOURTEEN (Location Map only, page 146)

Fricourt German Cemetery and Baron von Richthofen

THE GROUND

There is a small lay-by where you can park your car next to the cemetery. The cemetery was begun by the French in 1920 as the battlefields north of the Somme River were gradually being cleared both of debris and dead soldiers. The bodies of German soldiers were brought to Fricourt from some 79 surrounding communes.

The graves are from those killed over almost the entire period of the war between late September 1914 and October 1918. Having established the cemetery, it was handed over in 1929 to the German War Graves Agency, who began work on the cemetery's landscaping and building of permanent architectural features.

All work ceased with the outbreak of World War Two in 1939 and it was not until 1966 that the Germans were able to return and finish the work, including erecting the metal crosses. There are a total of 5,056 marked burials, plus 11,970 in mass graves at the rear of the cemetery.

Some of the black crosses mark up to four burials, intermingled with the headstones marking Jewish graves.

The German-Jewish organizations had enthusiastically backed the Kaiser and more than 100,000 German Jews enlisted in the

Fricourt German Cemetery - the metal crosses often with four names interspersed with Jewish graves.

German Army in 1914 alone and 12,000 subsequently gave their lives.

In the aftermath of war, as Germany became gripped in ever more virulent anti-Semitism, the defeat was blamed on the Jews. In 1935 Joseph Goebbels announced that it was forbidden to list the names of fallen Jews on memorials for the fallen of the First World War. He said a Jew who had fought in German uniform could not have been a real German and any working for the civil service were dismissed and deprived of citizenship.

I find these Jewish gravestones particularly moving, bearing in mind the treatment that the Jews were to receive both after the War and from the German Nazis in the Second World War.

BARON MANFRED VON RICHTHOFEN

In 1925 Baron Manfred von Richthofen was buried at Fricourt only to be removed to his family home in East Germany the following year. Richthofen was born into the Prussian nobility. After attending the local school he began military training at age eleven, on completion of which he joined a Prussian cavalry regiment.

When World War I broke out, Richthofen served on both the Eastern and Western Fronts. However, the Germans quickly concluded that traditional cavalry were obsolete due to machine guns and barbed wire. They converted their cavalry into infantry. Richthofen immediately transferred to the Imperial German Army Air Service, the forerunner of the Luftwaffe.

Richthofen was initially an observer, flying on reconnaissance missions over the Eastern Front. In 1915 he managed to shoot down a French aircraft with his observer's machine gun, but was not credited with the kill, as it fell behind Allied lines.

He then trained as a pilot. In April 1916 he downed a further French aircraft behind the French lines at Verdun. Again he gained no official credit. After a further spell flying two-seaters, he was selected for a newly formed fighter unit and won his first aerial combat over France in September 1916.

In November 1916, he downed his most renowned adversary, the British ace, Major Hawker, VC, for whom he had enormous respect as a fighter pilot. After this engagement, he was convinced he needed a fighter aircraft with more agility, even though this was at the sacrifice of speed.

He switched first to the Albatross (it was this plane which was first painted bright red) and then the following year to the celebrated Fokker triplane, the distinctive three-winged aircraft with which he is most commonly associated.

In January 1917, after his sixteenth confirmed kill, Richthofen received the the Blue Max, the highest military honour in Germany at the time. That same month, he assumed command of his own squadron, which ultimately included some of the elite of Germany's pilots, whom he trained himself.

Contrary to popular imagination, he was not a spectacular or acrobatic pilot. Rather than engage in risky tactics like his brother, who was credited with 40 victories, Richthofen exercised a set of flight principles to achieve the greatest success for both squadron and individual fighter pilots.

However, in addition to being a fine tactician and leader, he was recognized as a superb marksman. He viewed his aircraft as merely a platform from which to fire his guns. He led by example and force of will rather than by inspiration. He was often described as distant, unemotional and humourless. As a practical aid to easy identification in the melée of air combat, Richthofen's own aircraft was painted entirely red. His squadron adopted his colours with various individual markings.

Richthofen led his new unit to unparalleled success, peaking during April 1917. In that month alone, he downed 22 British aircraft, raising his official tally to 52. By June, he was the wing commander of the first of a new, larger formation. These were highly mobile units that could be sent at short notice to different parts of the front as required. The name 'The

Manfred Albrecht Freiherr von Richthofen, the Red Baron, (2nd May 1892 to 21st April 1918)

Flying Circus', came from both the unit's highly mobile nature (including the use of tents), and from its brightly coloured aircraft.

On 6th July 1917 Richthofen sustained a serious head wound. He was forced to land and was grounded for several weeks. Although Richthofen, by now known as the Red Baron, returned to combat in October 1917, his wound caused lasting damage. He suffered from post-flight nausea and headaches, as well as a change in temperament.

In 1918, Richthofen had become such a legend that it was feared that his death would be a blow to the morale of the German people. Richthofen himself refused to accept a ground job, stating that if the average German soldier had no choice in his duties, he would continue to fly in combat.

Each time he shot down an adversary, he ordered a silver cup to be engraved with the date of the fight and the type of enemy machine from a jeweller in Berlin. He continued this tradition until he had 60 cups, by which time the supply of silver in blockaded Germany was restricted.

Richthofen was killed on 21st April 1918, while flying over the Somme River when in combat with a young Canadian pilot. He was hit by a single .303 bullet almost certainly fired by Australian troops on the ground. He was alive on landing but died almost immediately. He had been a pilot for three years and had 80 victories to his name.

PLACE FIFTEEN (Map G, page 154)

Kiel Trench and Siegfried Sassoon's Military Cross

THE GROUND

From the crossroads just south of Fricourt, take the small lane up the hill and through the woods. As you come out on the southern side, turn left on the farm track and park up.

The German front line known as the Kiel Trench ran though the centre of the wood which was known as Bois Français. The British front line more or less followed the front of the wood. The two front lines were accordingly very close and there were a number of craters, although the situation on the ground today has been complicated by activity during the Second World War and what I assume to be some gun emplacements.

Sassoon was based in a dug-out close to the main road to your south west at 71 North. This position was connected by a communication trench to Battalion Headquarters at Maple Redoubt, which was just to the west of the cemetery you see to your south.

SIEGFRIED SASSOON

Sassoon was born in the Weald of Kent. He was brought up by his artistic mother, his parents having separated, and educated at Marlborough before going up to Clare College, Cambridge. Although he had a love of the countryside, horses, fox hunting, cricket and later golf, his real love and ambition was to be a poet. His sheltered, privileged and carefree world produced a kindly, unprofessional, humour-loving, observant but basically childlike being.

Sassoon was commissioned into 1st Bn. Royal Welch Fusiliers and arrived in France in November 1915. He was 28 years old. Robert Graves (author of *Goodbye to All That*), who had recently fought with the Regiment at the Battle of Loos, was already in the Officers' Mess. Graves tending to be outspoken, over-strung and self-conscious, was not particularly popular in the Mess, either with his peers or his superiors.

The two men discovered they shared similar literary interests and a friendship was struck up which, with one or two ups and downs, lasted throughout their lives. Both men were particularly fond of a young fellow officer, 2nd Lt David (Tommy) Thomas, with whom Sassoon had shared rooms at Pembroke College, Cambridge the year before. In a series of officer casualties, three officers were killed within a space of 24 hours on 18th March 1916, including Thomas.

Sassoon took Thomas's death to heart. His reaction was to take on dangerous duties, especially patrol work. He started going on two-man patrols into No Man's Land with an experienced and highly regarded Non-Commissioned Officer, Corporal O'Brien, with the sole aim of killing Germans.

Sassoon was quickly christened Mad Jack within the Battalion. The Commanding Officer sensed that all was not well and sent Sassoon off on a course at the Army School at Flixecourt.

In May he rejoined the Battalion on this section of the front. On the 25th there was a raid on Kiel Trench and Sassoon wrote a farewell letter

home, left it with his batman, took his nail-studded cosh, left his dug-out at 71 North and joined the raiding party in the next door dug-out where they were blackening their faces with burnt corks.

At 10.30pm they took the communication trench, Canterbury Avenue, up to Battalion Headquarters at Maple Redoubt, where Sassoon asked for permission to accompany the raid. To his disappointment he was ordered to stay behind and ensure that the raiders returned into the lines safely. His friend Lt. Norman Stansfield was to lead the raid.

During the day a gap had been cut in the British wire and the German wire had been 'strafed' by trench mortars to allow easy access. There were two mine craters just in front of the British front line. They were about 50 yards in diameter and over 25 feet deep with water at the bottom. Between the two craters was a narrow earthen bridge with the main German front line about 60 yards further on.

The objective of the raid was to cross between the craters, via the earthen bridge, enter the German front trenches by the enemy loop in front of the left hand crater, follow the two sides of the loop up to the main

Guards' Cemetery, Lesboeufs, (below).

trench, examine the short section of trench that they would have cut off, capture prisoners, bomb dug-outs and kill Germans.

The raid entered No Man's Land at midnight and Sassoon followed, leaving the communication trench and crawling up to the lip on the left hand crater with his evacuation party. The raiding party consisted of Stansfield, five NCOs including O'Brien, and 21 men. The raid was a failure. The wire was not properly cut, the Germans heard them coming and as they reached the enemy's wire, a fire-fight broke out. The raiders, caught in an exposed position close to the German front line, beat a hasty retreat.

Sassoon counted fourteen men safely home and then went further out and found Stansfield wounded and learnt that O'Brien was somewhere in the craters. Under enemy fire, Sassoon first descended into the left-hand crater and worked his way around at the bottom, but without finding O'Brien. He then clambered over into the right hand crater where he discovered the corporal. He was badly wounded and unable to walk, let alone climb up the steep sides to safety. Sassoon returned to the British lines and collected a couple of helpers and some rope. Mercifully the Germans stopped firing at them and they managed to bring O'Brien back and lower him over the British parapet into the British trench. Sadly, O'Brien was dead.

SIEGFRIED SASSOON, FROM 'THE COMPLETE MEMOIRS OF GEORGE SHERSTON'

A stretcher-bearer bent over him and then straightened himself, taking off his helmet with a gesture which vaguely surprised me by its reverent simplicity. O'Brien had been one of the best men in our Company. I looked down on him and then turned away. The face was grotesquely terrible, smeared with last night's burnt cork, the forehead matted with a tangle of dark hair.

Corporal O'Brien is buried in the Citadel New Cemetery to the south. (During the war the site of this cemetery was a large camp, first tented and later hutted, with an Advanced Dressing Station.)

Sassoon was awarded the Military Cross. Unlike many, Sassoon and Graves both survived the war and became highly successful authors.

PLACE SIXTEEN (Map G, page 154)

Mansel Copse and the Devonshire Cemetery

THE GROUND

Park your car in the small parking area and walk back to the top of the slope so that you can look half left over the narrow valley where you will see a small white shrine, which is in the village cemetery. The wood behind you was known as Mansel Copse.

The front line here was L-shaped, having originally been along the rear edge of the L-shaped copse. The largest section of the wood and the main axis of advance was actually to the north west along the line of the road.

The modern shrine close to the position of the original.

The Somme Battlefield

CAPTAIN DUNCAN MARTIN, LT. WILLIAM HODGSON, MC AND THE
REVD. ERNEST CROSSE, DSO
The Devonshires occupied this part of the front prior to the attack on 1st
July 1916. They had very much made it their own, not least by naming
the wood after one of their officers, Mansel-Cary, who had been killed by
a rifle grenade in April of that year.

At the very front of the wood was a lone tree which, unlike all the
other trees, had never been hit by artillery fire and, even more strangely,
supported a magpie's nest. The soldiers took a keen interest in the nest
and earlier in the year had watched a brood being successfully hatched,
nurtured and taking to the air.

One of their Company Commanders, Captain Martin, who was a professional artist, had carefully considered the ground in front of his position. He became convinced that a machine gun position at the base of a
shrine in the village cemetery was likely to inflict severe casualties on
any attack, unless it could be neutralized beforehand by artillery or mortars.

While on leave, he went to the trouble of making a plasticine model of
the Brigade Area to illustrate the contours of the ground and the inherent
dangers. The model was of such good quality and so accurate that it was
used for briefing all officers in the Brigade prior to the attack.

Unfortunately, the gun position was not destroyed and as Martin and
his troops left the area of the copse and began their advance, they were cut
down by the machine gun. Captain Martin and most of his command fell,
although the shrine was cleared by the Devonshires and the adjacent
Gordons later that afternoon.

Another officer in the Devonshires who died that day was Lt. William
Hodgson, MC, known as 'Smiler'. He was a popular and talented soldier,
the son of the Bishop of St. Edmundsbury and Ipswich and a graduate of
Christ Church, Oxford. He was already an established author (writing
under the name of Edward Melbourne). Two days before the attack he
had published a poem *Before Action* in which he refers to the hill on
which Mansel Copse stands and anticipated his own death.

The last lines of the poem read:

> *I, that on my familiar hill,*
> *Saw with uncomprehending eyes*

A hundred of Thy sunsets spill
Their fresh and sanguine sacrifice,
Ere the sun swings his noonday sword
Must say goodbye to all this;
By all delights that I shall miss,
Help me to die, O Lord.

The padre to the Devonshires was a man called Revd Ernest Crosse, DSO. Yet another Oxford man, having been educated at Balliol College, he had attended Ely Theological College before being ordained in 1912. Three days after the attack, Crosse went out on to the battlefield and collected 161 bodies of the Devonshires. He found nearly all of them by the tree with the magpie's nest. He brought them back and buried them in what had been their front trench.

I like to think that it was this man who went on to become the Chaplain at Marlborough College who came up with the wonderful words now engraved in stone at the entrance to the cemetery: 'The Devonshires held this trench. The Devonshires hold it still.'

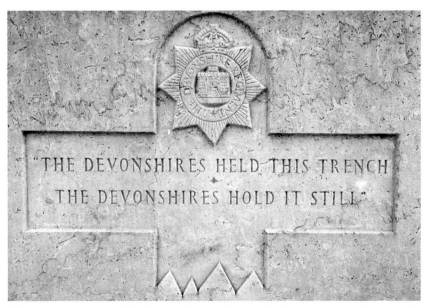

The stone plaque which has replaced the original wooden version, at the entrance to the cemetery.

PLACE SEVENTEEN (Map H, page 155)

Success with Gas, Flames, Mines and Footballs north east of Carnoy

THE GROUND

Park your car by the track on the right hand side of the road. You are in No Man's Land with the British lines behind you to the south and the Germans in front of you to the north. It was along this section of front line trenches that the British had released gas over the German lines towards Montauban during the pre-attack bombardment at the end of June 1916.

Directly in front of you to the north, you will see the remnants of mine craters, a remnant of activity typical of positions where the fronts were so close. A short distance to the left (west), a number of Russian Saps had been dug well out into No Man's Land which concealed underground a machine gun post, several mortar pits and a new secret weapon in the form of two massive Livens flamethrowers. (Mortars are a simple tube barrel weapon which can be used to fire bombs at a high angle over a short distance.)

Further to the west, the enemy line projected forward and was known as Casino Point. Further away to the right is a strip of woodland (known as Talus Boise), which almost exactly denotes the half way point from where you are standing to the junction with the French troops to the east.

The East Surreys occupied the trenches about 300 yards this side of the northern end of the wood. The village of Montauban is just over a mile to the north east.

The story here is largely of success, partly because the area was more lightly held but also because of the effective prior bombardment, the imaginative use of mines and good leadership.

GAS AND CAPTAIN WILLIAM LIVENS, MC

The French Army was the first to use gas, adopting a tear gas grenade from the beginning of the war. The Germans first used a chemical irritant against the British at Neuve Chapelle in October 1914. These weapons were not considered to represent a breach of the Hague Treaty of 1899, which prohibited projectiles containing asphyxiating gas.

At the second battle of Ypres in April 1915, Germany fired a deadly chlorine gas at the British for the first time. It produced a greenish smoke and a strong odour. The first attack caused casualties but the gas was fairly easy to detect and, being water soluble, could be countered by covering the mouth and nose with a damp or urine impregnated cloth. The first gas masks were quickly designed and issued.

Britain was incensed by what it considered an illegal and cowardly form of warfare but nonetheless responded by developing its own gas capability. Initially the British focused on the release of gas from canisters downwind of enemy positions (as they had here) but this policy was sometimes disastrous when the wind changed or enemy shelling ruptured the canisters within the British lines.

One British officer who was motivated into action by the German use of gas and the sinking of the *Lusitania* with the loss of 1,100 lives was a Royal Engineer called Captain William Livens, MC. (He had at first thought his fiancée had been killed when the ship went down but in fact she was not on board.) He was highly inventive, imaginative and determined.

His first significant invention was a massive two and a half ton flamethrower, known as the Livens flame projector, which he had tested at Wembley sports ground. He had installed four of these monsters underground, to the front of the British trenches close to the crest of the hill above Mansel Copse (one of these has recently been recovered and is now in the museum in Peronne). A further two were here, on the west side of the road. These devices were used in the attacks on 1st July 1916.

Despite this success, the devices were too heavy and required excessive ground preparation for frequent use, so Livens turned his attention to creating a simple mortar which could deliver canisters of oil over large distances to explode on impact. His prototype came into use three weeks later. Encouraged by this initial success and with the support and encouragement of General Gough, Livens further developed and refined what became known as the Livens Projector to fire canisters of gas up to 1,300 yards. Initially used at both Thiepval and Beaumont-Hamel in the autumn attacks, the Livens Projector became the preferred means by which the British Army delivered chemical attacks for the remainder of the war.

Chemical warfare had a large psychological impact but a limited killing capacity because whilst the type of gas used became more effective (with the best known being mustard gas), it was generally easy to detect and the quality and effectiveness of gas masks advanced in parallel. The gas tended to be fatal only in large doses so that despite extensive use, only 8,100 Empire troops are thought to have died from gas as against almost 200,000 gas casualties. As a result, whilst the use of gas increased over the course of the war, its overall effectiveness diminished.

CAPTAIN WILFRED PERCY (BILLY) NEVILL, CARNOY MILITARY CEMETERY E-28

Educated at Dover College, where he excelled at sport, he went up to Cambridge, only completing his first year before joining up in November 1914. He was actually commissioned into the East Yorkshire Regiment but he served on the front with 8th East Surrey Regiment as the Company Commander of B Company.

Nevill was something of an eccentric. He used to entertain himself, and no doubt his soldiers, by standing on the fire step in the front trench at night and yelling obscenities at the Germans! Nevill had concerns about maintaining both his men's morale and their momentum when they went 'over the top.' Accordingly, when he went on leave before the Big Push, he purchased four footballs, one for each of his platoons, to follow during the attack. He obtained his Commanding Officer's permission to issue the balls, on condition that the men were told not to run after them!

Each of the four balls were separately inscribed: the Great European Cup Final, The East Surreys v Bavarians, Kick off at Zero and No referee! Nevill offered a prize to the first platoon who kicked their ball into the German trenches.

THE ATTACK

At Zero hour Nevill kicked off leading one of the platoons. His B Company objective was the third line of German trenches which were close to the road running west from Montauban. The artillery bombardment was

116

Aerial photograph of a British gas attack in progress between Carnoy and Montauban (Place 17) in June 1916. Photograph by kind permission and copyright of Imperial War Museums.

largely successful. It was heavier than elsewhere and was supported by additional, loaned, heavy French artillery which smashed the deep German dug-outs. Furthermore, the wire was mainly well cut and the front line trenches were only lightly held.

During the night before, the turf covering the Livens flame projector nozzle, an underground machine gun emplacement and the mortar pits had been pushed aside. At Casino point at 7.27am (just before the attack), a 5,000lb charge at the head of a Russian Sap had been fired creating a crater 55 feet wide and 12 feet deep. This detonation was quickly followed by two smaller charges in what had been the tunnel, which helped create an open trench into the crater, along which troops could advance under cover before the attack began.

To a similar end, a number of what were called 'push pipe' mines were detonated which created linear craters up to 70 yards long and six feet deep into No Man's Land as a form of instant communication trenches, giving safe cover to the troops advancing.

A further mine was also blown under the German lines destroying three dug-outs, four sniper posts and a machine gun and a number of smaller 10-50lb mines were blown, which created 'man holes' which could be instantly occupied by machine gunners and mortar teams supporting the attack. The Livens flame projectors squirted their three, ten second shots of petrol (each consuming a ton of fuel) into the German positions, killing all those within range, scorching and terrifying others.

MAJOR GENERAL FOULKES

At Zero hour the two jets appeared to a height of two or three feet above the ground, opposite the German trench lines and well within the range of the machines: the automatic lighters functioned perfectly, and with a roar the streams of oil became ignited and shot forward towards the enemy, being traversed slowly from side to side, whilst dense clouds of black smoke, flecked with flame, rose a hundred feet into the air. No living thing could possibly survive under this visitation. A machine gun detachment emerged from another mine gallery on one side and sprayed the enemy trenches with bullets as our infantry were crossing No Man's Land and a mine was blown on the other side. It was not surprising that our infantry met with no opposition at this point.

Further east, away from Casino Point and the Livens flame projectors, the Germans held their positions more successfully and a machine gun was able to deliver enfilade fire over both the Queens and Nevill's East Surreys, who were adjacent.

Nevill was never to present his prize for the first football in a German trench because at the second line of trenches, the attack was held up by wire entanglements and as Nevill ran forward, he was shot through the head.

The momentum of the attack was maintained. The Surreys and other Battalions in the attack took their objective and two of the balls were recovered. The incident was widely reported in both the British and German press.

The British claimed it showed courage and strength of character.

The Germans considered it was an example of British madness!

PLACE EIGHTEEN (Location Map only, page 146)

Crucifix Corner: the Cavalry and Aircraft Attack at High Wood

(Bois des Forceaux)

THE GROUND

You will find the Crucifix in the centre of a small stand of trees at the T-junction. Turn to the right (east) and park by the track leading up to the left (north east). Walk up the small incline along the track so that you can see the fields in all directions.

To your left (west) is the small hamlet of Bazantin whilst to your right is the village of Longueval, beyond which is Delville Wood. To your north east, down the track about 1,500 yards away, is High Wood.

The battle for High Wood's 75 acres started on 14th July and raged nearly continuously for 64 days. During those two months, the Germans furiously repelled or counter-attacked every British assault. It came to be known as 'The hell of High Wood' and 'The rottenest place on the Western Front'. In the end, the British finally managed to overwhelm the Germans on 15th September 1916, though the commanding British General, Major-General Barter, was relieved of command four days later for 'wanton waste of men'.

It was the last of the big woods to be captured by the British and it is estimated that 10,000 British and German soldiers still lie unrecovered and unmarked under the canopy of the trees.

CAVALRY

Cavalry had been historically, and were initially, considered an essential offensive element of any military force. The shock on defenders of a mounted cavalry charge was well known but because horses could move faster and further over a battlefield than infantry, they were also a useful resource for scouting out the enemy, harrying his advance or disrupting his retreat.

Today, it is easy to ridicule the concept of horses and men armed with swords and lances charging soldiers armed with modern firearms. Perceptions in 1916 were different. During the retreat from Mons in August 1914, the 12th Lancers and the Scots Greys had charged a squadron of the Prussian Dragoons. They had charged uphill. Their lances and swords accounted for over 70 dead Germans at a cost of only five British deaths. Bearing in mind that attack is normally more costly than defence, this was a remarkable result.

It is even more remarkable when one also considers that some of these deaths were as a result of soldiers being shot in the back by Germans who, only seconds before, had put their hands up to surrender as the horses reached them, had then picked up their rifles again as the horses swept past. It may be for this reason that only four prisoners were taken.

In addition, the British cavalry were trained to kill not only with the sword and lance but also with the rife and machine gun. They were often supported with field guns of the Royal Horse Artillery. Horses were no less bullet proof then men. These troops could quickly be despatched over the battlefield and once dismounted, and the horses held in dead ground out of sight of the enemy, could put down small arms fire much more quickly than could be achieved by infantry. In truth they were the fore-bears of today's mechanised infantry.

General Haig was a cavalry officer and had always perceived that once the German front had been broken, the British cavalry could sweep through, harrying the retreating enemy and maintaining the momentum of the attack.

It has been estimated that over two million horses and mules served the British Army during the First World War and that more cargo space was used on shipping during the war for horses, horse fodder and support-ing materials than for any other purpose by a margin of about seven.

Better bred horses were generally found to suffer from shell shock and act up more when exposed to the sights and sounds of war than less-well-bred animals, which often learned to lie down and take cover at the sound of artillery fire.

Unlike men, breaks to horses' legs or other major injuries inevitably led to the animals being destroyed. Whilst British casualty rates for troops were around 10% killed of all those who served, for horses it was closer to 25% and there were times during the war when up to 1,000 horses would be arriving in France each day to replace those which had been lost.

Losses were typically due to artillery fire, disease and exhaustion, with some horses drowned in only ankle-deep mud, too tired to lift their heads high enough to breathe. If commanders are to be criticised for the use of cavalry, the criticism should be aimed not at the concept and place for cavalry on the battlefield but the fact that they were almost always deployed too late, as happened at High Wood. The battle opened with a Divisional attack which included a combined British and Indian cavalry charge. This is the story of the charge on 14th July 1916.

THE CHARGE

At 9am that morning the British had taken the Bazentin villages. The Germans had been taken by surprise. To the north east across the shallow valley was High Wood, commanding one of the highest points on the battlefield, beyond which lay the incomplete German third line. The possibility of a breakthrough at last seemed possible. There was no sign of the enemy and the standing corn in front of the wood and a lack of wire defences suggested good going for cavalry.

The 2nd Indian Cavalry Division – made up of 7th Dragoon Guards and the 20th Deccan Horse supported by the 34th Poona Horse – had been held in readiness to exploit a breakthrough. They were encamped at Morlancourt, four miles south of Albert. They had been ordered forward at 7.40am but owing to the churned up nature of the battlefield, by midday had only reached Carnoy. They were halted whilst their orders were reviewed. Finally, in the evening, almost twelve hours after they had set off and ten hours after the initiative had been conceived, they arrived at Crucifix Corner.

The Germans had lost no time. They had already regrouped after the set-backs of the early morning and had begun filtering back into the wood and, in particular, fortified a strong trench known as the Switch Line. This was a long, deep and heavily manned position which ran from Martinpuich, along the valley, through the north east corner of High Wood and out beyond it, cutting a scar across open country, to pass behind the equally strongly fortified Delville Wood, eventually forming a bastion in front of the village of Flers further north.

Stone markers naming the avenues through Delville Wood.

In addition, as soon as the local German General got news of the arrival of the British Cavalry, he sent all his reserve divisions into the area with orders to hold the British and then counter-attack, thus thwarting any possibility of the intended break-through.

The attack was mounted from here at around 8pm. The infantry attacked the south western face of High Wood on foot, while the cavalry charged across the fields, uphill towards the eastern boundary and the area south of it facing Longeval village.

The charge was supported by the cavalry machine guns and although artillery fire as well as intense machine gun and rifle fire from the rein-forced German defenders, in and outside High Wood, harried their approach, the machine gun, which had opened up from Longueval vil-lage, was quickly silenced by British guns.

Before reaching the wood the 7th Dragoons, who led the charge, had speared sixteen Germans and captured another 32 who, terrified by the ferocity of the attack, surrendered. The Deccan Horse killed more and captured a further six. After this success they came under machine gun fire from German soldiers hiding in the cornfield and from snipers in Delville Wood to their east.

The crew of a British two-seater aircraft saw the cavalry's predicament and whilst the pilot took the aeroplane over the German machine gun post, his observer fired his Lewis gun into it. Having located the position, the aircraft over-flew a Royal Horse Artillery battery and dropped a mes-sage bag over the side of the aircraft to the gunners below containing a sketch of the site. With this information they were able to subject the machine gunners to accurate supporting fire.

Despite this, the cavalrymen realised that any further advance would be suicidal. They had dismounted, fought into the wood and subsequent-ly dug themselves in against counter-attacks. They successfully held their positions during the night against the counter-attack which began at mid-night, and were withdrawn early the next morning a little after 3am.

They took their own wounded with them. Some were carried away on blankets slung between lances. Other cavalrymen walked, their horses having been lamed. Fortuitously, a mist descended, making the morning darkness even more impenetrable, and the survivors disappeared unseen to the safety of the rear areas.

One can speculate what might have happened if the cavalry had been brought up in time to charge at nine in the morning as soon as the opportunity was seen but despite this, the cavalrymen suffered fairly lightly, with ten dead, 91 wounded and three missing. The horses had suffered more – 43 horses were killed outright, 103 were wounded and fifteen went missing.

Mounted cavalry was to take no further part in the Somme battles of 1916 but there were charges elsewhere and the 7th Dragoon Guards completed their last charge crossing the River Dendre in Belgium as the clocks struck 11am on 11th November 1918.

Delville Wood, the South Africans and Post Traumatic Stress Disorder

THE GROUND

There is a public car park at the west end of the wood with public conveniences.

The memorial with the wide avenue bordered by a double row of oak trees was designed by Sir Herbert Baker and inaugurated in 1926. The museum is inspired by the Castle of Good Hope in Capetown. It was built in the mid 1980s and commemorates South Africa's entire military history for all of its three services. It is intended to symbolize the unity of the English and Afrikaans speaking people of South Africa and represents the national symbol for bravery and sacrifice. It was opened by President Botha in 1984.

The woods have been replanted and the rides are marked with stone markers with the names given to the avenues during the fighting, as well as one memorial which marks a hornbeam, which is the only tree which survived the battle. The woods have never been cleared of the dead and it remains the burial ground of those who fell there.

THE SITUATION ON 15TH JULY 1916

The wood was a major German defensive position which the South Africans were tasked with taking on 15th July 1916.

The assault began with a fearsome artillery bombardment, followed by an assault by the South Africans on an axis from the south west to the north east. However Waterlot Farm (due south of the cemetery on the next road) remained in German hands, meaning that they faced the enemy on three sides.

Over the following five days there was fierce and confused hand to hand fighting amongst remnants of the trees and the shell damaged trenches. Some German snipers even worked their way behind the attackers, concealing themselves amongst the high branches of trees. Throughout this period it rained every day and the Germans continuously bombarded the wood with rates of fire at times in excess of 400 shells a minute.

The only tree which survived the battle.

The wood was transformed into a chaotic jungle of interwoven splintered trees and undergrowth overlying muddy shell holes filled with water, littered with the wounded, dead and dying of both sides. Although the South African orders were to take the wood at all costs, they were both outflanked and outnumbered. When they were finally relieved on 20th July, initially only 142 men of the original 3,150 came out of the wood unscathed. Eventually 780 men assembled.

The wood was finally captured on 25th August 1916 by 14th Light Division, only to be overrun by the Germans in March 1918 and finally taken again by 38th Welsh Division on 28th August 1918.

Waterlot Farm was not captured until August 1916, when the German trenches were occupied by the Royal Fusiliers, who suffered losses from 'friendly fire'. Their regimental doctor, who witnessed men being buried alive and watched the desperate efforts of their mates to dig them out, was Captain Wilson.

CAPTAIN CHARLES MCMORAN WILSON, MC

Charles Wilson was born at Skipton-on-Craven in Yorkshire, where his father was the local doctor. He was educated at Pocklington Grammar School and decided he wished to become a writer, but took his father's advice that medicine would give him a more secure future.

He entered St Mary's Hospital, Paddington in 1902, the same year as Sir Alexander Fleming, and quickly demonstrated by his editorship of the hospital *Gazette* and by captaining the hospital rugby fifteen, that he was a man with a decisive mind and exceptional determination.

He had high standards but was not always easy to please and he became disillusioned with some of his teachers. He decided to take a break from medicine and went abroad to study art in Florence and Rome before taking a post looking after an elderly American widow on the Upper Nile. In 1913 he returned to St Mary's in London, took his MD, was awarded the gold medal in medicine and appointed medical registrar.

On the outbreak of war he enlisted in the Royal Army Medical Corps and was posted as medical officer to 1st Battalion the Royal Fusiliers. He spent two years in the front line enduring the hardships of trench warfare and giving himself a first-hand insight into mental trauma. He was awarded the Military Cross in 1916 and twice mentioned in despatches.

He was later appointed as Winston Churchill's personal doctor, for which he was ennobled as Lord Moran of Manton. In 1945 he published a book called *The Anatomy of Courage*. It is dedicated, 'To my father who was without fear, by his son who is less fortunate.'

His book is based on the recollections of his experiences at the front during the First World War and shows how perceptive and sensitive he was about the difference between fear and cowardice.

Late in 1914 he had examined a sergeant who was 'out of sorts'. The man had a reputation for being imperturbable on patrol and a steadying influence on younger and less experienced soldiers. He now sat in his billet, staring at the fire, unshaven, slovenly dressed and silent. The doctor could find nothing wrong with him but gave him permission to rest until the Battalion came out of the trenches.

The following day, when everyone else had gone up to the line, the sergeant blew his own head off. At the time Wilson thought little of it. The accepted view at that time was that battle experience hardened men into seasoned veterans, but the sergeant's death kept coming back to haunt him.

As the war progressed, he began to observe carefully both the behavior of those under his care, the psychological process of scarring and the birth of his own fear. He noticed that few men could bear more than three weeks in the front line without becoming jumpy, and regular tours of the trenches caused many men to try and drown the war in whisky.

He came to the conclusion that men wore out like old clothes. Everyone possessed a different level of courage which he described as 'credit'. Some men might only have £500 on which to draw, others many thousands of pounds. Different aspects of war demanded various outlays, but everything had a price: relentless exposure to the wet, mud and cold, cost; the loss of friends, cost; while bombardment or battle demanded serious expenditure. Men were continually drawing down on their account; no one had unlimited funds and when a man's capital was used up, he was finished, but this did not make him a coward.

Wilson was probably the first person to come up with an explanation for the cause of what today we know as Post Traumatic Stress Disorder (PTSD). It is now accepted that PTSD can manifest itself in numerous ways but it is often accompanied by change of character and mental instability. These changes frequently lead to service men and women leaving the services before their illness has been recognized or diagnosed.

Sometimes a worsening of their condition leads to crime and violence and it is of interest and concern that a recent estimate has suggested that there may be as many as 8,500 ex-servicemen in prison out of a total prison population of 92,000 (which is over 9%).

Whatever the correct statistic as far as PTSD in prison may be, two things are known. First, soldiers are notoriously reluctant to seek help for mental illness and during this delay, their condition worsens. The average period between leaving the services and seeking help from charities such as

Delville Wood commemorated on the Thiepval Memorial.

Combat Stress is fourteen years. Second, the drain on the total credit of courage, as Moran called it, has been higher in Afghanistan than in any conflict in which this country has immersed itself since World War Two.

PLACE TWENTY (Map I, page 156)

Ginchy, the First use of Tanks, the death of the Prime Minister's Son and the end of a Future Prime Minister's War

THE GROUND

Park your car by the side of the road close to where the power lines cross the road. Perhaps one of the most visited graves on the Somme is that of Raymond Asquith, the then Prime Minister's son, which is in the Guillemont Road Cemetery (I-B-3). Visited rather less is the scene of the Guards' attack on 15th September, the historic day when tanks were used in battle for the first time and the place where Asquith was mortally wounded.

The stark and featureless ground over which the Guards attacked and where Asquith was mortally wounded.

The ground here is flat and featureless and illustrates the difficulty advancing troops would have experienced in terms of trying to find and keep their bearings during an attack. It was even more so in September 1916, having been torn up by shell-fire over the previous months, first British as they attacked and then German as they withdrew. On top of this, because the British were advancing, they had none of the familiarity with the ground from which they had benefited in the initial stages of the attack.

The Guards Division was to attack from the remains of the village of Ginchy in a broadly north easterly direction towards a German trench line called Straight, about 700 yards to the east. At the northern and southern ends of Straight trench there were two strong-points, known as the Triangle in the north and the Quadrilateral in the south. This second feature was seen as a particular threat to the attack and accordingly it was decided that it would be assaulted by a brand new invention in the form of tanks, moving ahead of the infantry from the south.

TANKS

As early as 1914 there had been proposals for armoured fighting machines. Caterpillar tracked vehicles which were used to move heavy guns and armoured cars, with little capacity to cover rough ground, were also common.

In September 1915 a Royal Engineer Officer called Ernest Swinton, who sat on the Imperial Defence Committee with Winston Churchill, recommended the development of what was later to be known as the tank. Kitchener was not taken with the idea but Churchill was. He duly recommended it to the Prime Minister, Herbert Asquith, who authorised the project.

The first prototype was demonstrated to Kitchener in January 1916. It had a rhomboidal form with the armaments at the side to provide a low centre of gravity and allow it to climb German parapets. There were to be two types. One was armed with a 6lb naval gun and several machine guns, known initially as Big Willie; while the other simply had machine guns and was called Little Willie. Following the demonstration, a hundred Big Willies were ordered. They weighed 28 tons, had armour plating about one third of an inch thick, a sixteen litre Daimler engine and were just over eight feet high. Top speed was under four miles an hour but steering them was difficult and they were also difficult to see out of or communicate from.

They were manned by a crew of eight in hot, noisy, fume-filled and cramped conditions. Commanders were sceptical as to how to deploy them to advantage and the crew training had been minimal. To protect the secrecy of the invention, they were given the deliberately misleading names of tanks.

LT RAYMOND ASQUITH

Raymond Asquith, the Prime Minister's eldest son, had been an outstanding pupil at Winchester, from where he won a scholarship to Balliol College, Oxford. His brilliance continued and he duly won the Ireland, Derby, and Craven scholarships and, to no-one's surprise, finished with a first class honours degree.

He was called to the Bar in 1904 and quickly established a reputation and a thriving practice. He was junior counsel to the investigation into the sinking of the *Titanic* and was considered as the potential Liberal candidate for Derby.

On the outbreak of war he obtained a commission into 16th (County of London) Battalion, London Regiment, but subsequently transferred to 3rd Battalion, Grenadier Guards. Initially on arrival in France he was detailed off for staff duties but he requested to be returned to active duty with his battalion, which was duly granted before the Battle of the Somme.

BACKGROUND TO THE ATTACK

Tactical thinking had progressed rapidly since the disasters of 1st July. The revised approach was to utilise two artillery bombardments simultaneously: a standing artillery barrage on the enemy's position and a creeping barrage, immediately behind which the troops would advance.

Two weeks before the attack, Asquith's Battalion had trained as part of the Brigade with this new tactic in mind. Asquith was decidedly unimpressed with this training, in which the creeping barrage was represented by the Regimental drummers. He concluded that the sight of four battalions, walking in lines at a funeral pace across cornfields preceded by a row of drummers, was more like some ridiculous religious ritual ceremony performed by an ancient tribe than a Brigade of Guards training for battle.

A week later the Prime Minister briefly visited the front and Asquith rode over to the crossroads in Fricourt to meet him. The Prime Minister was pleased by everything he saw and appeared delighted that there was some localised shell-fire which justified him taking shelter in an old German dug-out in the village.

Lt. Raymond Asquith

THE ATTACK

The night before the attack was fine and clear with a full moon and the Battalion left their bivouacs at Carnoy and marched to Ginchy via Guillemont. They arrived at 3am and formed up in assembly trenches 100 yards east of the village (which were dug by linking up shell holes) to avoid any likely shelling of the village. Sandwiches and an issue of rum were served to the men, who then tried to sleep. In the background they heard for the first time the strange noise of tanks which had been allocated to the attack, moving up behind them.

In total 35 tanks were deployed that day over the entire front. The very first tank on the battlefield started from a point 200 yards west of Ginchy and advanced towards the eastern end of Delville Wood (where it was quickly knocked out by artillery fire).

A total of nine tanks were ordered to support the Guards. Three were to attack along the line of the road to Lesboefs, three were to attack the eastern end of the Triangle and three were to attack the Quadrilateral from the south. At 6am British heavy guns fired a short salvo of about 40 shells which woke up the enemy, who responded by shelling Ginchy (in particular the northern end). Fifteen minutes later orders were passed down the line to fix bayonets and the attack started five minutes later.

Asquith's Battalion was to share the lead of the Brigade attack with 1st Battalion Coldstream Guards on their right. Asquith was to lead No 4 Company on the left hand side. Almost immediately on standing up for the attack, No 4 Company was met by machine gun fire and Asquith was shot through the chest and mortally wounded. All the officers of this

Company were killed within 200 yards of their own trenches and only five officers in the Battalion survived the battle unscathed.

According to one of his soldiers, "there is not one of us who would not have changed places with him if we had thought that he would have lived, for he was one of the finest men who ever wore the King's uniform, and he did not know what fear was."

He was carried back to a shell-hole where there was an improvised dressing station. There they gave him morphia but he died an hour later.

The difficulty with the attack was maintaining the right direction. The forming up trenches were facing east, rather than north east, which was to be the line of attack. It proved difficult to stay in touch with the Brigade to their west and they were unfamiliar with the terrain, which was featureless. Finally they had to contend with the creeping barrage ahead of them and the enemy shells falling all around.

Very soon after the start of the attack, about 250 yards from the start line, the advancing troops came across an unexpected line of intermediate

trenches. In truth, these were little more than connected shell holes but they served to shelter a number of Germans equipped with machine guns who fought with the utmost bravery. The guns had not bombarded them and the creeping barrage had passed over them too quickly to do much harm. Every German holding these intermediate lines was immediately either shot or bayonetted.

The advance then ran into further difficulties. 6th Division on the right had failed to advance and were still just outside Ginchy, meaning that their flank was completely exposed. As the

Guards took their objective (the Straight trench), they were enfiladed with machine-gun fire from the south and shelled, taking heavy casualties, including the Commanding Officer and most of the other officers.

Only one of the nine promised tanks had made the start line but the Artillery had carefully left 100 yard gaps in the barrage to allow the far larger number of tanks to advance. Without the tanks and without an effective creeping barrage, the results were deeply felt.

Unfortunately, in the confusion of the battlefield, with its limited visibility and unreliable compass within the steel shell, the one tank which remained operational went too far to the west, missing its objective of the Quadrilateral, and continued to the north where the Germans opened fire with armour piercing ammunition normally used against snipers hidden behind metal shields. Both the driver and one of the gunners were hit by splinters. Wary of the machine being captured, the commander withdrew back to the British lines to the south.

By evening, the Battalion held a small frontage at the southern end of their first objective but they were subjected to repeated bombing attacks and efforts by the enemy to work around their position. Fire steps were cut into both sides of the trench, with fighting continuing throughout the night and all counter-attacks being repulsed. The Battalion was finally relieved on the evening of 16/17th September and the remainder of Straight Trench was finally taken the next day.

Whilst the use of tanks in this attack was considered something of a non-event or even an unnecessary evil, they were meeting greater success in the village of Flers to the west. Here twelve tanks, which had started from the ground to the west of Delville Wood, reached the German Front line and eleven of these reached the southern end of Flers. Six were successful in penetrating beyond the village and the British press reported that one tank went boldly right through the village, down the main street, firing as it went, followed by parties of cheering infantry.

THE NEWS REACHING HOME

From *Margot Asquith Autobiography* (1920)

On Sunday, 17th September we were entertaining a weekend party, which included a number of our family and friends. While we were playing tennis in the afternoon my husband, Henry went for a drive with my cousin, Nan Tennant. He looked well, and had been delighted with his visit to the front and all he saw of the improvement in our organization there: the tanks and the troops as well as the guns. Our Offensive for the time being was going amazingly well. The French were fighting magnificently, the House of Commons was shut, the Cabinet more united, and from what we heard on good authority the Germans more discouraged.

While we were playing games Clouder, our servant came in to say that I was wanted. I left the room, and the moment I took up the telephone I said to myself, 'Raymond is killed'. With the receiver in my hand, I asked what it was, and if the news was bad. Our secretary, Davies, answered, "Terrible, terrible news. Raymond was shot dead on the 15th. Haig writes full of sympathy, but no details. The Guards were in and he was shot leading his men the moment he had gone over the parapet."

I put back the receiver and sat down. I heard my daughter Elizabeth's delicious laugh, and a hum of talk and smell of cigars came down the passage from the dining-room. I went back into the sitting-room.

"Raymond is dead," I said, "he was shot leading his men over the top on Friday." Puffin got up from his game and hanging his head took my hand; Elizabeth burst into tears, I walked away with the two children and rang the bell:

"Tell the Prime Minister to come and speak to me," I said to the servant. Leaving the children, I paused at the end of the dining-room passage; Henry opened the door and we stood facing each other.

He saw my thin, wet face, and while he put his arm round me I said: "Terrible, terrible news." At this he stopped me and said: "I know... I've known it... Raymond is dead." He put his hands over his face and we walked into an empty room and sat down in silence.

THE END OF A FUTURE PRIME MINISTER'S WAR

Later in the day on 15th September a further Brigade of the same Guards Division fought their way further north towards the Triangle.

HAROLD MACMILLAN

Harold Macmillan was born in Chelsea, London. His family owned the well known publishing house which had been founded by his grandfather, who was the son of a Scottish crofter.

He was taught classics from the age of six and subsequently attended Eton before going up to Balliol College Oxford, where he took a first class degree. His American mother, who was both protective and ambitious, played an important part in Macmillan's life.

He joined the Grenadier Guards which his mother, who was sensitive about the family's commercial and humble background, considered socially acceptable. He took part in the offensive at Loos in September 1915 where he was shot through the right hand. He was evacuated to hospital and although it was not a serious wound, he never recovered the strength of that hand, which affected the standard of his handwriting. It was also responsible for what became known as his 'limp handshake'. He returned to the Western Front in April 1916.

He was lightly wounded for a second time in July 1916 while leading a three man night patrol near Ypres.

They challenged us, but we could not see them to shoot, and of course they were entrenched while we were in the open. So I motioned to my men to lie quite still in the long grass. Then they began throwing bombs at us at random. The first, unluckily, hit me and the blast stunned me.

The German responsible was attacked by Macmillan's corporal who summed up his actions, "I 'it 'im, and 'is 'elmet came off. I 'it 'im again, and the back of 'is 'ead came off!"

By the end of the month Macmillan had moved with his battalion to Beaumont-Hamel. He wrote to his mother that, "the flies are again a terrible plague, and the stench from the dead bodies which lie in heaps around is awful."

Macmillan's 4th Grenadier Guards objective was the Triangle. They advanced under German bombardment through Ginchy but with their own creeping barrage ahead of them. Fortunately, the ground was wet and soggy and numerous German shells failed to explode. Despite this, Macmillan was slightly wounded by a shell splinter just below the knee.

As they left the village, they realized that they had lost contact with two Coldsteam Battalions which they assumed, wrongly, were ahead of them and had already taken the Triangle. After a wait, they continued their advance, found the Triangle still in enemy hands and after a short but vicious struggle succeeded in capturing and occupying the front trenches. It was at this point that they came under fire from a machine gun about 500 yards away to the west. Macmillan was ordered to silence it.

He described to his mother what happened to him:

The German artillery barrage was very heavy, but we got through the worst of it after the first half-hour. I was wounded slightly in the right knee. I bound up the wound at the first halt, and was able to go on. About 8.20 we halted again. We found that we were being held up on the left by Germans with a machine gun which was very tiresome. It was about 500 yards away in an uncleared trench.

I was taking a small party across to the left with a Lewis gun, half crouching and half crawling to try and get into this trench without being seen, when I was wounded by a bullet in the left thigh just below the hip, from about 30 yards away. It was a severe wound, and I was quite helpless. I rolled into a shell-hole, shouted to Sgt. Robinson to take command of my party and go on with the attack.

Although the machine gun was knocked out, he remained in the shell hole throughout most of the remainder of the day, effectively stranded in No Man's Land whilst fierce fighting continued all around. He dosed himself with morphine and in his lucid moments read *Prometheus Bound* in the original Greek. Periodically he saw Germans running around the lip of his shell hole and he lay doggo hoping none of them would join him!

In the evening he was found by his Company Sergeant Major, who physically carried him back to the Serpentine Trench, close to the Triangle, from where he was taken by stretcher bearers to the dressing station in Ginchy with another less badly wounded officer. They arrived to find the station had been abandoned, but thinking that others would have a more urgent need, they sent the stretcher bearers back to the front and continued on their way by supporting each other.

Unfortunately, the Germans began bombarding the village again and in the confusion, the two officers became separated. Macmillan managed to stagger out of the village before collapsing in a ditch. He was eventually found and evacuated from there by men of the Sherwood Foresters.

Because of the length of time it had taken before he was given proper medical care, combined with the primitiveness and lack of modern drugs in First World War hospitals, the wound closed up and abscesses formed inside, poisoning his whole system.

Harold Macmillan, 1915.

Macmillan was returned to England and for a while his life seemed to be in danger. His pain was so bad that over the next two years, he had to submit to anaesthetic each time his dressings were changed. He recovered but he never returned to the front and walked with a limp for the rest of his life. His wartime bravery meant he later became known as Supermac and was regarded with admiration by his fellow soldiers. In total he was wounded five times.

Conclusion

THE BATTLE OF THE SOMME officially ended on 18th November 1916. Since the disasters of 1st July, a further 90 attacks had been made. Lessons had been learned and commanders at all levels, as well as the troops themselves, had become more experienced and effective.

The territorial objectives of 1st July had been substantially achieved but so too was the tactical objective of reducing the pressure on the French at Verdun, with the Germans more than doubling their deployment of troops on the Somme before the end of July.

GENERAL CARTON DE WIART

We had two great assets which the Germans could not emulate. The unconquerable spirit of the British who are at their best when they are losing and an unfailing sense of humour which can rise above everything else.

It also illustrated that Great Britain was prepared to match the losses which had already been sustained by the French, and it heralded the arrival of the tank which, in time, would ensure that the ghastliness of trench warfare would be consigned to history.

The final cost was over 200,000 dead and a million wounded or missing. Some suggest that this was a terrible waste. They are mistaken. This was the awful price of freedom.

By the end, for most soldiers, the war had become the enemy, not the Germans.

Useful Addresses

Somme 1916 Museum
Rue Anicet Godin
80300 Albert
Tel: 00 33 (0)3 22 75 16 17

Museum of the Great War
Chateau de Peronne, BP20063,
80201 Peronne
Tel: 00 33 (0)3 22 83 14 18 or email: info@historical.org
Open every day from 10am to 6pm

Thiepval Visitor Centre
8 Rue de l'Acre,
80300 Thiepval
Tel: 00 33 (0)3 22 74 60 47

Newfoundland Memorial Park
Tel: 00 33 (0)3 22 76 70 86
email: newfoundland.memorial@vac-acc.gc.ca

Best Western Hotel Royal Picardie
138 Avenue du Général Leclerc
80300 Albert
Tel: 00 33 (0)3 22 75 37 00 or email: reservation@royalpicardie.com

Bibliography

Soldiers, Richard Holmes, Harper Press, 2011

Famous 1914-1918, Richard van Emden and Victoria Piuk, Pen & Sword Military, 2008

Happy Odyssey, Lt. General Sir Adrian Carton de Wiart, Jonathan Cape 1950.

The Somme Battlefields, Martin and Mary Middlebrook, Penguin Books 1994

The first day on the Somme 1 July 1916, Martin Middlebrook, Penguin Books, 1984

Somme, Lyn Macdonald, Penguin Books, 1993

Memoirs of an Infantry Officer, Siegfried Sassoon, Faber & Faber, 1997

The Anatomy of Courage, Lord Moran, Constable & Robinson, 2007

The Tricks War Plays, Christopher Robbins, Slightly Foxed, Autumn 2008.

Somme 1916 a battlefield companion, Gerald Gliddon, The History Press, 2009

Major and Mrs Holt's Battlefield Guide to the Somme, Leo Cooper, 2003

From Leicestershire to the Somme, Aubrey Moore, Unpublished

'It's Only Me,' A life of the Reverend Theodore Bayley Hardy VC, DSO, MC, David Raw, Frank Peters Publishing Ltd, 1988

Last Man Standing, Richard van Emden, Pen & Sword Books, 2002

Tommy, Richard Holmes, Harper Collins, 2004

An Autobiography, Margot Asquith, Penguin Books, 1920

Siegfried Sassoon and the Great War, The Making of a War Poet, Dennis Silk

Lutyens and the Great War, Tim Skelton and Gerald Gliddon, Frances Lincoln Ltd, 2008

The Times, 14 July 2013, Don't judge the Great War by what came later, Ben MacIntyre

The Somme, Peter Barton, Constable & Robertson, 2006

The Maps

SECRET

NOT TO BE TAKEN BEYOND

BRIGADE HEADQUARTERS

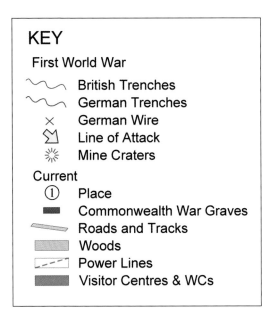

KEY

First World War

~~~ British Trenches
~~~ German Trenches
× German Wire
Line of Attack
Mine Craters

Current
① Place
Commonwealth War Graves
Roads and Tracks
Woods
Power Lines
Visitor Centres & WCs

NOTE:
The Location Plan, on page 146-7, is an extract from the French 'Bleue de IGN' series, © IGN - 2014, authorisation no. 80-1430.

The maps on pages 148-56 are reproduced by kind permission and copyright of The National Archives of the UK, except Map B of Rossignol Wood which is by the author.

Additions and amendments to reflect modern features to all the following original trench maps are copyright of the author.

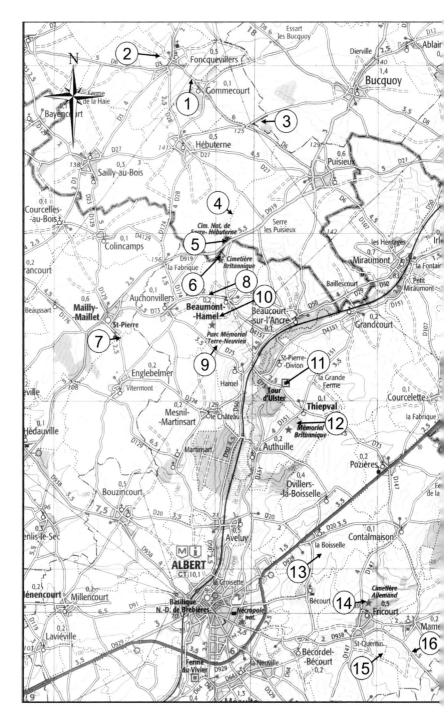

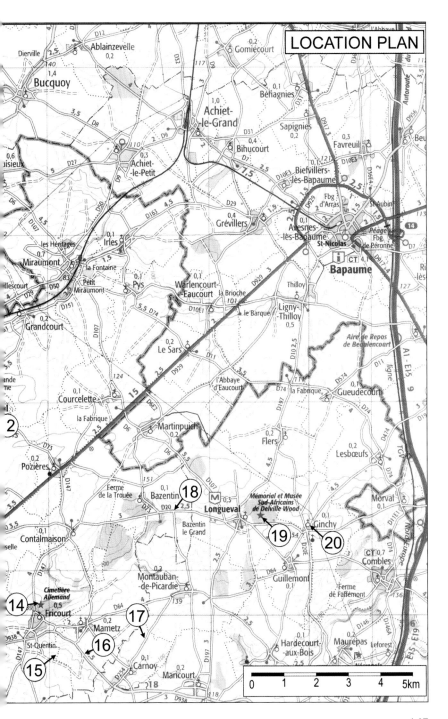

LOCATION PLAN

147

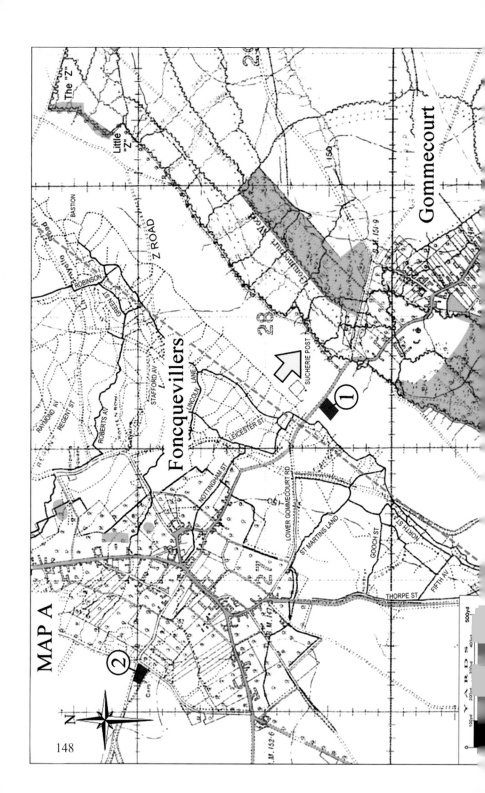

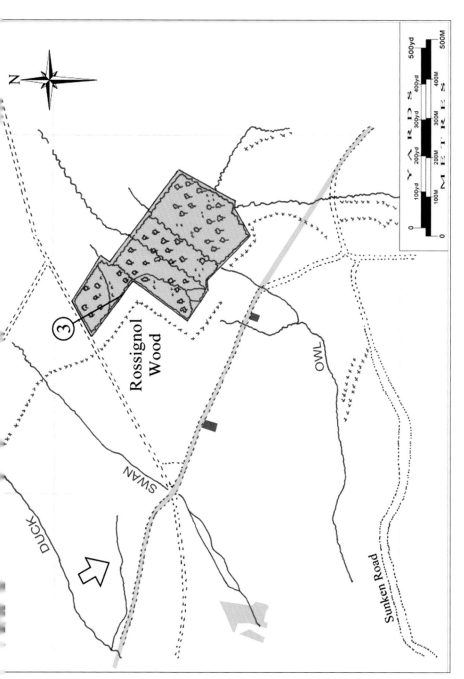

N

Rossignol
Wood

SWAN

DUCK

OWL

Sunken Road

YARDS
0   100yd 200yd 300yd 400yd 500yd
METRES
0   100M 200M 300M 400M 500M

③

149

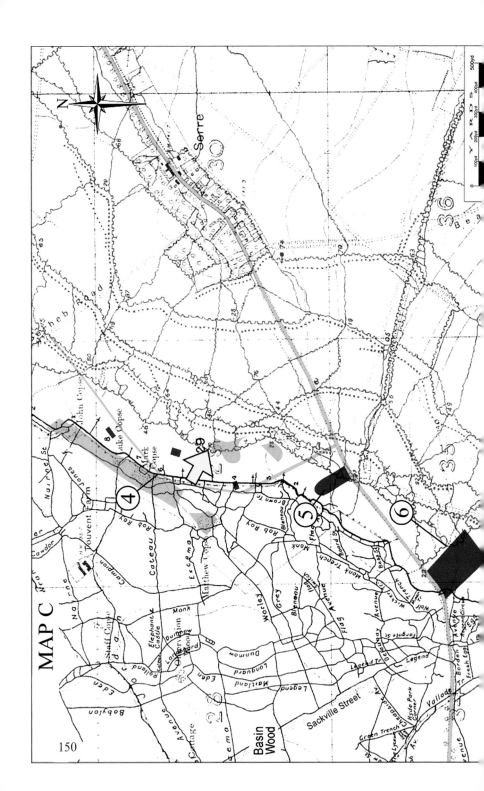

MAP C

N

Serre

Basin
Wood

150

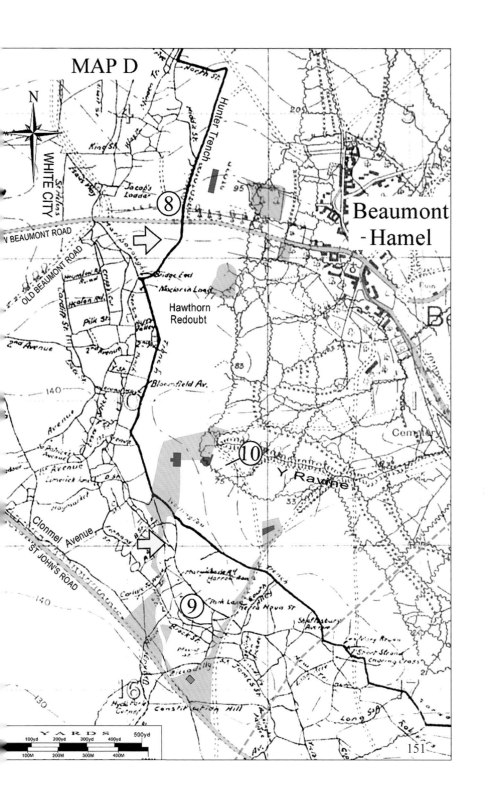

MAP D

N

WHITE CITY

King St

St Helens

Jacob's Ladder

Hunter Trench

North St

⑧

NEW BEAUMONT ROAD

OLD BEAUMONT ROAD

2nd Avenue

Pilk St

Cardiff St Hill

2nd Avenue

Bridge East

Mailboth Load

Hawthorn Redoubt

Bloomfield Av.

95

83

Beaumont -Hamel

B

140

Avenue

Avenue

Limerick Road

Haymarket

⑩

Y Ravine

Cemetery

33

Clonmel Avenue

ST JOHN'S ROAD

140

⑨

Park Lane

Nova St

Shaftesbury Avenue

Charing Cross

⑥

130

Hyde Park Corner

Brock St

James St

Piccadilly

Constitution Hill

Long Sap

YARDS
100yd 200yd 300yd 400yd 500yd
100M 200M 300M 400M

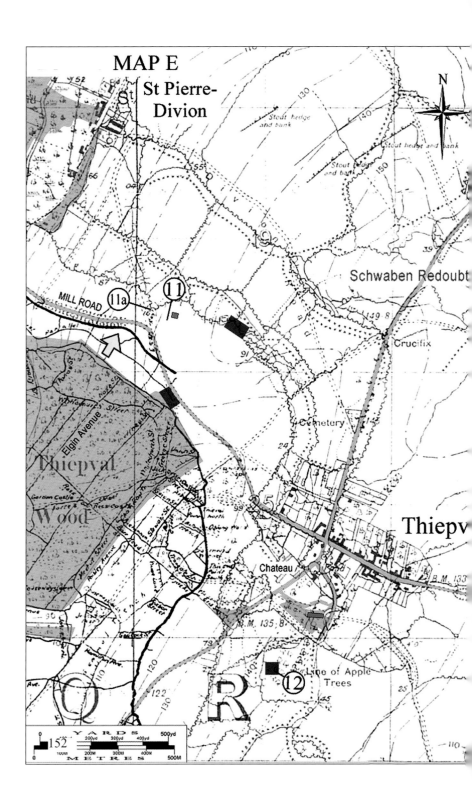

MAP E

St Pierre-
Divion

N

Stout hedge
and bank

Stout hedge and bank

Stout hedge
and bank

Schwaben Redoubt

MILL ROAD

11a   11

Crucifix

Cemetery

Elgin Avenue

Thiepval

Wood

Thiepv

Chateau

B.M. 135.8

Line of Apple
Trees

12

Q

R

152

Y A R D S
200yd   300yd   400yd   500yd
M E T R E S
100M   200M   300M   400M   500M

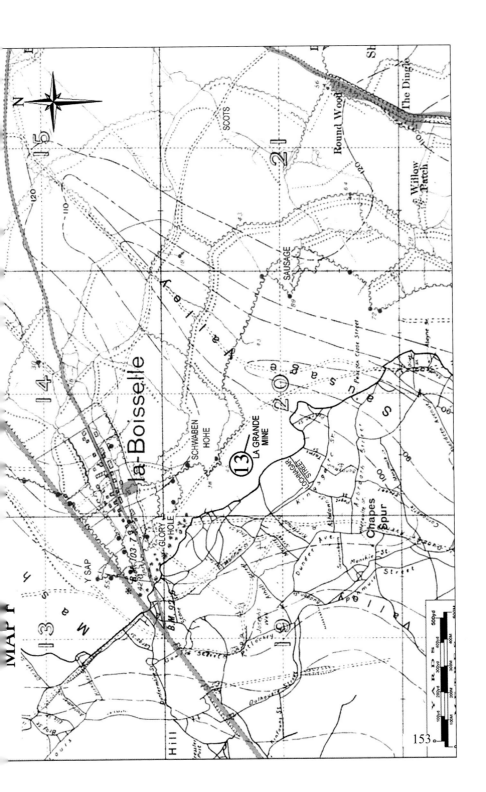

MAP F

153

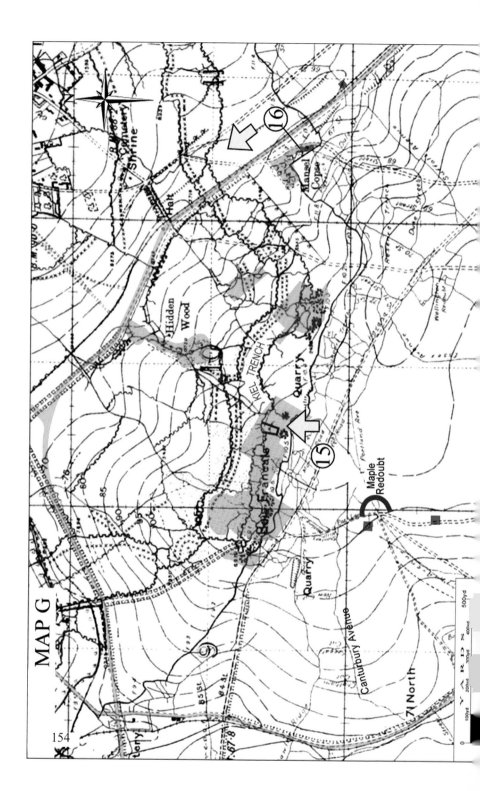

MAP G

154

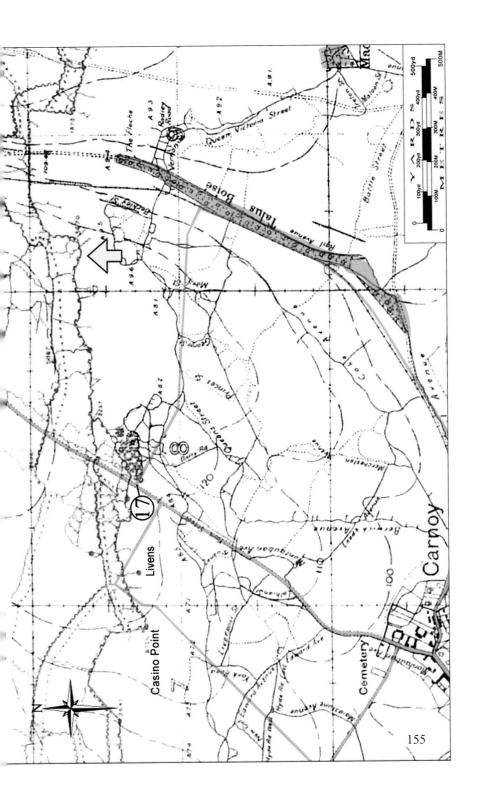

155

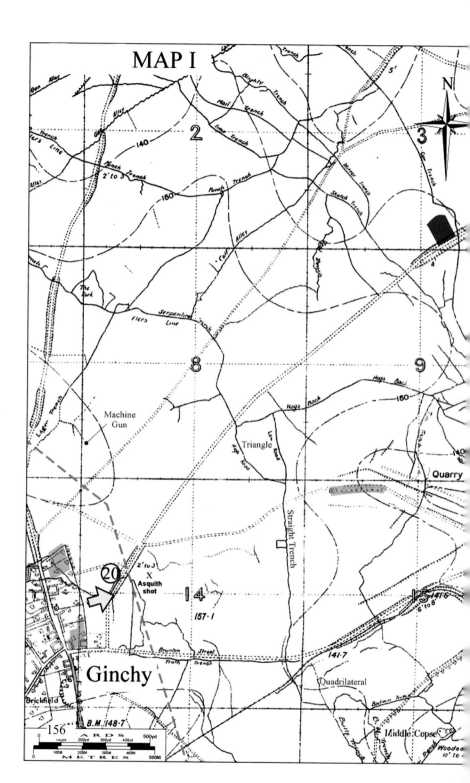

MAP I

N

156

B.M. 148·7

Ginchy

Brickfield

Quarry

Quadrilateral

Middle Copse

Machine Gun

Triangle

Straight Trench

Asquith shot

About the Author

Ruaraidh Adams-Cairns was brought up on the North East coast of Scotland. He was educated at Gordonstoun and Reading University, where he read Estate Management, followed by the RMA Sandhurst. He joined the Queen's Own Highlanders (Seaforth and Camerons) and served in Germany, Scotland, Gibralter, Belize and Northern Ireland. For the last 34 years he has worked for Savills, the international firm of Chartered Surveyors. He lives in London but one day hopes to return to Scotland.